W9-BFN-136

Animals

**Titles in the
Discovering Careers
series**

**Adventure
Animals
Construction
Nature
Sports
Transportation**

Animals

Ferguson
An imprint of Infobase Publishing

Animals

Copyright © 2010 by Infobase Publishing

Ferguson
An imprint of Infobase Publishing
132 West 31st Street
New York NY 10001

Library of Congress Cataloging-in-Publication Data

Animals.
    p. cm. — (Discovering careers)
  Includes bibliographical references and index.
  ISBN-13: 978-0-8160-8044-1 (hardcover : alk. paper)
  ISBN-10: 0-8160-8044-5 (hardcover : alk. paper) 1. Animal industry—Vocational guidance—Juvenile literature. 2. Animal culture—Vocational guidance—Juvenile literature. 3. Veterinary medicine—Vocational guidance—Juvenile literature. 4. Zoology—Vocational guidance—Juvenile literature. 5. Animal specialists—Vocational guidance—Juvenile literature. I. Infobases, Inc.
  SF80.A55 2010
  636.0023—dc22
                    2009034905

Ferguson books are available at special discounts when purchased in bulk quantities for businesses, associations, institutions, or sales promotions. Please call our Special Sales Department in New York at (212) 967-8800 or (800) 322-8755.

You can find Ferguson on the World Wide Web at http://www.fergpubco.com

Text design by Erika K. Arroyo and Erik Lindstrom
Composition by Mary Susan Ryan-Flynn
Cover printed by Bang Printing, Brainerd, Minn.
Book printed and bound by Bang Printing, Brainerd, Minn.
Date printed: September 2010
Printed in the United States of America

10 9 8 7 6 5 4 3 2 1

This book is printed on acid-free paper.

CONTENTS

Introduction

You may not have decided yet what you want to be in the future. And you don't have to decide right away. You do know that right now you are interested in animals. Do any of the statements below describe you? If so, you may want to begin thinking about what careers involve working with animals.

____ Science is my favorite subject in school.

____ I am responsible for feeding and caring for our family pet.

____ I enjoy visiting the zoo.

____ I regularly watch television shows about animals and nature.

____ I am concerned about endangered species.

____ I collect butterflies/insects.

____ I enjoy caring for horses.

____ I like to read stories about animals.

____ I enjoy bird watching.

____ I often visit the aquarium.

____ I belong to a 4-H Club or the National FFA Organization.

____ I like to groom my dog or cat.

____ I always volunteer to watch my neighbor's dog when he goes on vacation.

____ I like to adopt stray animals.

____ I like to teach my dog new tricks.

____ My parents are farmers and I would like to continue the family business.

____ I like to hike in the woods and watch animals in the wild.

Discovering Careers: Animals is a book about careers involving animals, from animal breeders and technicians to zoologists. People who work with animals help us better understand our environment. They study, care for, raise, train, and protect species, from amoebas to primates.

This book describes many possibilities for future careers working with animals. Read through it to see all of the options that are available. For example, if you are interested in working with pets such as dogs, cats, and birds, you will want to read the chapters on Animal Shelter Workers, Pet Groomers, Pet Shop Workers, and Pet Sitters. If you are interested in caring for and protecting wild animals, you will want to read the chapters on Fish and Game Wardens, Marine Biologists, Zoo and Aquarium Curators and Directors, Zookeepers, and Zoologists. If you are not sure what type of animals you want to care for, then you should read the chapters on Animal Caretakers, Veterinarians, and Veterinary Technicians. Perhaps you like to take photographs of animals. If so, then you'll be interested in reading the article about Wildlife Photographers. Go ahead and explore!

What Do Animal Workers Do?

The first section of each chapter begins with a heading such as "What Animals Trainers Do" or "What Veterinarians Do." It tells what it's like to work at this job. It describes typical responsibilities and assignments. You will find out about working conditions. Which animal workers work inside in offices or laboratories? Which ones work outside in all kinds of weather? Which ones work on boats in the ocean or in humid jungles? What tools and equipment do they use? This section answers all these questions.

Education and Training

This section tells you what classes and education you need for employment in each job—a high school diploma, training at a junior college, a college degree, or more. It also talks about on-the-job training that you could expect to receive after you're hired and whether or not you must complete an apprenticeship program.

Earnings

This section gives the average salary figures for the job described in the chapter. These figures provide you with a general idea of how much money people with a particular job can make. Keep in mind that many people really earn more or less than the amounts given here because actual salaries depend on many different things, such as the size of the company; the location of the company; and the amount of education, training, and experience you have. Generally, but not always, bigger companies located in major cities pay more than smaller ones in smaller cities and towns, and people with more education, training, and experience earn more. Additionally, federal agencies—such as the National Park Service or U.S. Fish and Wildlife Service—pay more than those at the state level. Also remember that these figures are current averages. They will probably be different by the time you are ready to enter the workforce.

Outlook

This section discusses the employment outlook for the career: whether the total number of people employed in this career will increase or decrease in the coming years and whether jobs in this field will be easy or hard to find. These predictions are based on economic conditions, the size and makeup of the population, foreign competition, and new technology.

Keep in mind that these predictions are general statements. No one knows for sure what the future will be like. Also remember that the employment outlook is a general statement about an industry and does not necessarily apply to everyone. A determined and talented person may be able to find a job in an industry or career with the worst kind of outlook. And a person without ambition and the proper training will find it difficult to find a job even in a booming industry or career field.

For More Info

Each chapter includes a sidebar called "For More Info." It lists organizations that you can contact to find out more about the field and careers in the field. You will find names, addresses, phone numbers, email addresses, and Web sites.

Extras

Every chapter has a few extras. There are photos that show workers in action. There are sidebars and notes on ways to explore the field, fun facts, profiles of people in the field, tips on important skills for success in the field, information on work settings, lists of Web sites and books, and other resources that might be helpful.

At the end of the book you will find three additional sections: "Glossary," "Browse and Learn More," and "Index." The Glossary gives brief definitions of words that relate to education, career training, or employment that you may be unfamiliar with. The Browse and Learn More section lists animal-related books, periodicals, and Web sites to explore. The Index includes all the job titles mentioned in the book.

It's not too soon to think about your future. We hope you discover several possible career choices. Happy hunting!

Animal Breeders and Technicians

What Animal Breeders and Technicians Do

Animal breeders and technicians help to breed, raise, and market a variety of farm animals. Other animal breeders work with domesticated animals kept as pets, such as song birds, parrots, and all dog and cat breeds. Even wildlife populations that are kept in reserves, ranches, zoos, or aquariums are bred with the guidance of a breeder or technician.

Breeders work to create better, stronger breeds of animals or to maintain good existing breeds. They are helped by techni-

EXPLORING

- Organizations such as 4-H Clubs (http://www.4h-usa.org) and the National FFA Organization (http://www.ffa.org) offer good opportunities for learning about, visiting, and taking part in farm activities. The American Kennel Club (http://www.akc.org) sponsors clubs dedicated to particular dog breeds. It also offers activities for young people. These clubs usually have educational programs on raising and breeding animals.
- Raising pets is a good introduction to the skills you need for this career. Learning how to care for, feed, and house a pet give you basic knowledge of working with animals.
- Talk to animal breeders and technicians about their careers.

cians. *Artificial-breeding technicians* collect and package semen for use in insemination. *Artificial insemination technicians* collect semen from the male species of an animal and artificially inseminate the female. Whether the breeding is done artificially or naturally, the goals are the same. *Cattle breeders* mate males and females to produce animals with desired traits such as leaner meat and less fat. *Horse* and *dog breeders* try to create more desirable animals. They want horses and dogs who perform well, move fast, and look beautiful.

Words to Learn

animal husbandry the breeding and care of farm animals; also called *animal science*

breeding the sexual pairing of two members of the same species for the purpose of producing offspring

corporate farm a farm owned and operated by a large company; animal breeding on corporate farms takes place on a large scale

domesticated animal an animal that has been kept and raised (and tamed) by humans; examples would include pigs, cattle, and dogs

insemination the introduction of sperm into the female uterus of a mammal or the oviduct of an egg-laying animal during breeding

offspring descendents of a plant or animal produced as a result of breeding

species a group of related organisms that are capable of breeding

wild animal an animal that has not been tamed by humans; examples would include bears, gorillas, and mountain lions

For nonfarm animals, breeders usually work with several animals within a breed or species to produce offspring for sale. There are ranches that produce a large number of exotic animals, and some stables and kennels that run full-staff breeding operations, but most pet breeders work out of their homes.

Most breeders and technicians who work on farms specialize in one of two areas. Those who specialize in livestock production work with cattle, sheep, pigs, or horses. Those who specialize in poultry production work with chickens, turkeys, geese, or ducks.

Tips for Success

To be a successful animal breeder or technician, you should

- be organized
- have love, empathy, and respect for animals
- have an interest in reproductive science
- have good communication skills
- be willing to continue to learn throughout your career

Education and Traning

Classes in math, biology, and chemistry will prepare you for a future career in animal breeding. Many animal breeders and technicians learn their skills on the job. There are also many colleges that offer two-year programs in animal science or animal husbandry. Students learn about feeds and feeding, agricultural equipment, and breeding techniques. They also study farm management and animal health. A high school diploma is almost always needed before you can enter these programs.

Earnings

The salaries of animal breeders and technicians depend on who the employer is, their educational and agricultural background,

FOR MORE INFO

For more information on becoming an animal breeder, contact
American Kennel Club
8051 Arco Corporate Drive, Suite 100
Raleigh, NC 27617-3390
919-233-9767
http://www.akc.org

For information on careers, contact
American Society of Animal Science
1111 North Dunlap Avenue
Savoy, IL 61874-9604
217-356-9050
asas@assochq.org
http://www.asas.org

For industry information, contact
National Cattlemen's Beef Association
9110 East Nichols Avenue, #300
Centennial, CO 80112-3425
303-694-0305
http://www.beef.org

the kind of animals they work with, and the area where they work. Animal breeders just starting out in the field earned less than $17,510 in 2007, according to the U.S. Department of Labor. Those with experience earned $26,000 to $54,000 or more. Technicians earn salaries that range from $15,000 to $40,000 a year.

Outlook

Technicians and breeders who have specialized skills and degrees from technical programs will find the most job opportunities. It is becoming harder for small farms to make money, so animal breeders and technicians will find most employment opportunities with large, corporate farms.

Animal Caretakers

What Animal Caretakers Do

Animal caretakers provide care to animals. There are many different kinds of animal caretakers. For example, *veterinary assistants* usually work with dogs and cats. *Wildlife shelter workers* work with all sorts of wild animals, from birds to bears.

Generally, animal caretakers feed the animals, clean their living spaces, exercise them, make notes and reports on the animals, and give attention and affection. They are trained to examine animals for signs of illness, such as lack of appetite, fatigue (tiredness), sores, and behavior changes. Animal caretakers keep the animals' living areas clean and safe. They provide stimulating

EXPLORING

- Learn more about animal laboratory care by visiting http://www.kids4research.org.
- If your family has a pet, offer to take responsibility for its care, including feeding, exercising, and grooming.
- Volunteer to work at animal shelters, pet stores, rescue centers, sanctuaries, zoos, or aquariums.

- Start a pet walking or sitting service in your neighborhood. This will give you an introduction to animal care. Be sure to only take on the number and kinds of animals you know you can handle.
- Talk to an animal caretaker about his or her career.

DID YOU KNOW?

Where Animal Caretakers Work

- Pet stores
- Kennels
- Stables
- Animal shelters
- Zoos
- Aquariums
- Laboratories
- Veterinary facilities
- Animal experimentation labs
- Federal government agencies (such as the U.S. Department of Agriculture and the Centers for Disease Control)
- State and local government agencies
- State and local parks
- Wildlife rehabilitation centers
- Pharmaceutical companies

activities, called enrichment activities, for the animals, such as playing with them or walking them.

In some jobs, animal caretakers take on greater responsibilities as they get more experience. They might give medication, trim nails or beaks, and train animals. Some caretakers do clerical work such as filing or record-keeping. Others do administrative work, such as screening people who want to buy or adopt a pet, writing care plans or reports, or talking with the animals' owners about care that has been given. The main job of animal caretakers, though, is to take care of the animals.

Tips for Success

To be a successful animal caretaker, you should

- be dependable
- be able to follow instructions
- have the ability to work on your own, when necessary
- love and respect animals
- be in good physical condition
- have good communication skills

Education and Training

To work as an animal caretaker, you must graduate from high school. In high school you should take classes in anatomy and physiology (the study of the structure and functions of living organisms), science, and health. Any knowledge of animal breeding, behavior, and health will also be helpful.

There are two-year educational programs in animal health. This type of program offers courses in anatomy and physiology, chemistry, mathematics, clinical pharmacology, pathology, radiology, animal care and handling, infectious diseases, biology, and current veterinary treatment. Graduates of these programs usually go on to work in veterinary practices, shelters, zoos and aquariums, pharmaceutical companies, and laboratory research facilities. A bachelor's degree in biology, zoology, or an animal-related field is required for some positions, especially those in zoos and aquariums.

Earnings

Animal caretakers earn an average of $19,000 a year, although their pay can range from less than $14,000 a year to more than $31,000. Animal caretakers who work for social advocacy

FOR MORE INFO

For information about animal laboratory work, contact
American Association for Laboratory Animal Science
9190 Crestwyn Hills Drive
Memphis, TN 38125-8538
901-754-8620
info@aalas.org
http://www.aalas.org

For more information on careers and other resources, contact
American Veterinary Medical Association

1931 North Meacham Road, Suite 100
Schaumburg, IL 60173-4360
847-925-8070
avmainfo@avma.org
http://www.avma.org

For industry information, contact
Pet Care Services Association
1702 East Pikes Peak Avenue
Colorado Springs, CO 80909-5717
877-570-7788
http://www.petcareservices.org

organizations such as animal shelters earn about $20,000 a year. Most positions require little training and as a result offer low salaries.

Outlook

The animal care field keeps growing. More and more people are becoming pet owners, so there is more need for veterinary care, boarding facilities, and grooming and pet shops. Much of the work is part-time. Many employers rely on volunteer workers, so competition is high for paid positions. The most desired positions are in zoos, aquariums, and wildlife rehabilitation centers, but those jobs are the hardest to find.

Graduates of veterinary technician programs will have the best chances of getting a job. Laboratory animal technicians and technologists will have especially good opportunities. Increasing concern for animal rights and welfare means that these facilities are staffing more professionals to work in their labs.

Animal Shelter Workers

What Animal Shelter Workers Do

Animal shelter workers work for nonprofit organizations. They protect animals and promote animal welfare. Most shelter workers care for small domestic animals, such as cats, dogs, and rabbits. Employees at some shelters also work with horses, goats, pigs, and other larger domesticated animals. The following paragraphs detail some of the major jobs in animal shelters.

Kennel attendants work most closely with the shelter animals. In addition to handling the animals, kennel attendants

EXPLORING

- Public libraries have books that give a detailed look into the world of animal shelters and humane societies.
- If you want to learn more about animal shelter work, contact a local shelter to inquire about humane education presentations that are scheduled in the community. You might attend these education sessions or an open house at the shelter.
- Some shelters might agree to allow you to spend a day following or working with a kennel worker.
- Volunteering at a shelter is the best way to learn about careers in animal shelters. Shelters usually welcome volunteers who are considering future careers involving animals.

An animal shelter worker examines a pit bull. (Brennen Smith, *The Decatur Daily*/AP Images)

check the health of animals, refer them for treatment when necessary, and keep records on them. Experienced attendants may be trained to give shots or medications under the supervision of a veterinarian.

Adoption counselors screen people who wish to adopt animals from the shelter. They must have good communication and judgment skills.

Animal control workers respond to calls about neglected or lost animals. They rescue injured animals and control stray and potentially dangerous animals wandering at large. They also bring lost pets to an animal shelter where their owners can reclaim them. Animal control employees sometimes work with local agencies, such as social services or law enforcement, to protect both people and animals.

Humane investigators follow up on reports of animal abuse and neglect. They interview witnesses and owners who are accused of mistreating animals. If investigators find that there has been abuse or neglect, they may call the police or take the animal away. Humane investigators also rescue stray or injured animals and take them to the shelter.

Humane educators work at the shelter and in the community. They teach people about the humane treatment of animals. They travel to schools, clubs, and community organizations to talk about animal treatment, animal rights, and other issues. They hand out educational materials and arrange tours of the shelter.

The First SPCA

The first American Society for the Prevention of Cruelty to Animals (SPCA) was started in 1866 through the efforts of Henry Bergh and other early crusaders for animal welfare. Not long after, Caroline Earle White and the Women's SPCA of Pennsylvania started the first truly humane animal shelter. Because of these two events, careers in animal shelter work began. Over the years, the focus of animal shelter work has changed from animal control to the welfare and humane treatment of animals.

Shelter managers hire, train, and supervise staff and oversee the maintenance of the property and equipment. Shelter administrators oversee the daily operation of the shelter. They select and hire kennel attendants, humane educators, humane investigators, and other shelter workers. They raise money to help pay for the operation of the shelter, attend community events, and recruit new members.

To be a successful animal shelter worker, you should have a deep love of animals and enjoy caring for them. You should also be able to work well with others. It takes a team of specialized workers—from kennel attendants and adoption counselors, to human educators and shelter managers—to keep a shelter running well. Additionally, many shelter positions involve inter-

DID YOU KNOW?

- There are between 4,000 and 6,000 animal shelters in the United States.
- Animal shelters care for six to eight million dogs and cats each year.
- Only 18 percent of owned cats and 10 percent of owned dogs are adopted from shelters.

Source: Humane Society of the United States

action with the public. Other important skills for animal shelter workers include the ability to work independently when necessary, patience, compassion, dedication, organization, and a strong work ethic.

Education and Training

You need a high school diploma or GED to work as a kennel attendant, adoption counselor, or animal control worker. Classes in anatomy and biology help prepare you for working with animals. Shelter managers frequently have a college degree, although experienced veterinary or shelter workers may be promoted into the position. Shelter administrators usually need a bachelor's degree and experience in business or shelter management.

Earnings

Salaries vary widely for animal shelter workers. Senior-level managers and other managers can earn, in some cases, more than $100,000 a year. Salaries for middle managers range from $20,000 to $50,000. Other workers may earn minimum wage to $30,000 or more a year.

Outlook

According to the Humane Society of the United States and the American Humane Association, the United States is in a pet-overpopulation crisis. According to the American Pet Products Association, there were 74.8 million dogs and 88.3 million cats in the United States in 2008. There are not enough qualified owners for all these animals. And in some instances, animals are being abused by their owners. As a result, employment of

FOR MORE INFO

The association works to protect both children and animals.
American Humane Association
63 Inverness Drive East
Englewood, CO 80112-5117
800-227-4645
info@americanhumane.org
http://www.americanhumane.org

For information on careers and training, contact
American Society for the Prevention of Cruelty to Animals
424 East 92nd Street
New York, NY 10128-6804
212-876-7700
http://www.aspca.org

Visit the society's Web site for information on stopping animal cruelty.
Humane Society of the United States
2100 L Street, NW
Washington, DC 20037-1525
202-452-1100
http://www.hsus.org

For information on animal protection and care, contact
National Animal Control Association
PO Box 480851
Kansas City, MO 64148-0851
http://nacanet.org

animal shelter workers should remain steady in coming years. There will be good jobs available for shelter workers due to the high turnover that results from hard work and low pay.

Animal Trainers

What Animal Trainers Do

Animal trainers teach animals to obey commands, compete in shows or races, or perform tricks to entertain audiences. They train dogs to protect property or work in law enforcement or to act as guides for people with disabilities. Animal trainers may

EXPLORING

- Learn as much as you can about animals, especially animal psychology.
- Volunteer to work in animal shelters, pet-training programs, rescue centers, pet shops, or veterinary offices. Also explore volunteer opportunities at zoos, aquariums, museums that feature live animal shows, and amusement parks. If you are interested in horses, you may find opportunities to volunteer at local stables.

- Try to teach your dog or cat tricks. Keep a journal of methods that are effective and those that are not.
- Talk to an animal trainer about his or her career. Ask the following questions: What made you want to become an animal trainer? What are your typical hours? What do you like most and least about your job? How did you train for the field? What advice would you give to someone who is interested in the career?

specialize in training one kind of animal or they may work with several types.

There are many animals that can be trained, but the same methods generally are used to train all of them. Animal trainers use a program of repetition and reward to teach animals to behave in a certain consistent way. To do this, they first look at the animal's temperament (personality) and aptitude (ability to learn) to see if it is trainable. Then they decide what methods to use to train it. They offer rewards, such as food treats or praise, to gradually teach the animal to obey commands. Animal trainers also feed, exercise, groom, and take general care of the animals they train.

How Do Animals Learn?

Most animal trainers use a method called *operant conditioning*. Operant conditioning teaches animals a particular behavior by offering a positive reinforcer. A positive reinforcer can be a treat, a toy, a back scratch, or anything that encourages an animal to repeat the desired behavior. For example, when you teach a dog to sit, you can reward its obedience with a treat or by saying "good dog!" Humans learn by operant conditioning, too. When your parents give you money (a positive reinforcer) for mowing the lawn, you are likely to mow the lawn again.

One of the most important and common examples of animal training is the companion animal to people with disabilities. These dogs are trained with several hundred verbal commands. For example, they must be able to walk their companions around obstacles on the sidewalk. Very few dogs pass the difficult companion dog training program. Dogs are now trained not only to help those who are blind or who can't see well, but also people who use wheelchairs, who have hearing impairments, or who have other physical disabilities.

Animal trainers usually specialize with one kind of animal. *Dog trainers* train dogs in companion programs, for police work, for performance in the entertainment industry, to

A dolphin trainer works with a dolphin alongside researchers and other trainers. (Steve Helber, AP Images)

protect private property, or to make them easier to control for their owners. *Horse trainers* train horses for riding or harness, or for shows, or the highly specialized field of racehorse training. Some horses are even trained to help people who have disabilities. *Police horse trainers* work with police horses to keep them from getting overly excited in crowds or responding to other animals (such as a barking dog) in their presence.

Some animal trainers work with more exotic animals for performance or for health reasons. A *marine mammal trainer* may teach dolphins or whales to roll over, lift their fins and tails, and open their mouths on command. These behaviors may be entertaining to aquarium visitors, but they serve a larger purpose. They allow zoo veterinarians to do a large amount of veterinary work without anesthesia, which is always dangerous for animals.

Education and Training

There are no special educational requirements for jobs in animal training. A few positions require a college degree. Animal trainers in circuses and the entertainment field are sometimes required to study animal psychology (the study of how animals think). Zoo and aquarium animal trainers usually must have a bachelor's degree in a field related to animal management or animal physiology (the study of the functions of living organisms). Trainers of companion dogs for people with disabilities prepare for their work in a three-year course of study at special schools.

Earnings

Salaries for animal trainers vary based on the type of animal they train, their experience, and their employer. Trainers just starting out in the field earn less than $16,000 a year. Those with many years of experience earn more than $48,000 a year.

DID YOU KNOW?

- Dogs that are trained to help blind or visually impaired people are called Seeing Eye dogs or dog guides.
- Only dogs that have been trained by The Seeing Eye organization can be called Seeing Eye dogs.
- Seeing Eye dogs typically work seven to eight years before being retired.
- Some Seeing Eye dogs are able to work until they are 10 or 11 years old.
- When Seeing Eye dogs are retired, they can be kept as pets by their owner, given to friends or family, or returned to the facility that trained them in the first place.

Source: The Seeing Eye

FOR MORE INFO

For information on careers and training, contact the following organizations:

Association of Zoos and Aquariums
8403 Colesville Road, Suite 710
Silver Spring, MD 20910-3314
301-562-0777
http://www.aza.org

Association of Pet Dog Trainers
150 Executive Center Drive, Box 35
Greenville, SC 29615-4505
800-738-3647
information@apdt.com
http://www.apdt.com

Canine Companions for Independence
PO Box 446
Santa Rosa, CA 95402-0446
800-572-2275
http://www.caninecompanions.org

Dogs for the Deaf
10175 Wheeler Road
Central Point, OR 97502-9360
541-826-9220
info@dogsforthedeaf.org
http://www.dogsforthedeaf.org

Outlook

Employment for dog trainers is excepted to be very good in coming years. More dog owners are seeking trainers to help their dogs learn how to behave. People with disabilities are also increasingly seeking out specially trained dogs and other animals to help them do daily tasks. Dog trainers will also be needed to train dogs that are used to sniff out bombs or illegal drugs in public places such as airports.

Employment for marine mammal trainers and horse trainers is not expected to be as good. These fields are small and employ only a few trainers.

Aduarists

What Aquarists Do

Aquarists work for aquariums, oceanariums, and marine research institutes. Their job duties are similar to zookeepers. Aquarists feed fish, maintain exhibits, and do research. They work on breeding, conservation, and educational programs.

Aquarists clean and take care of tanks every day. They make sure pumps are working. They check water temperatures, clean

EXPLORING

- Read books about oceans, animals, and careers in the field. Here are a few suggestions: *National Geographic Encyclopedia of Animals*, by Karen McGhee and George McKay (National Geographic Children's Books, 2006); *Oceans*, by Beverly McMillan and John A. Musick (Simon & Schuster Children's Publishing, 2007); and *Opportunities in Marine Science and Maritime Careers*, by William Ray Heitzmann (McGraw-Hill, 2006).

- Watch nature shows on television.
- Ask your parents to help you set up an aquarium. Do research before you start collecting fish. Learn how to operate equipment, feed and care for the animals, and provide a healthy environment for them.
- Visit your local zoos and aquariums often. Learn about the various species of aquatic animals and observe how they are exhibited.

DID YOU KNOW?

Dolphins are the most popular marine animals at aquariums. Here are other favorites (in descending order):

- sharks
- tropical fish
- killer whales
- sea turtles
- seals
- sea lions
- coral exhibits

Source: Alliance of Marine Mammal Parks and Aquariums

glass, and sift sand. Some exhibits have to be scrubbed. Aquarists also change water frequently and vacuum tanks routinely. They water plants in any marsh or pond exhibits. Food preparation and feeding are important tasks for aquarists. Some animals eat live food, but others eat cut-up food mixtures. Some animals need special diets prepared.

Aquarists carefully observe all the animals in their care. They must understand their normal habits, including courtship, mating, feeding, social habits, sleeping, and moving, and be able to judge when something is wrong. Aquarists write daily reports and keep detailed records of animal behavior.

Many aquarists collect and stock plants and animals for exhibits. They may have to make several trips a year to gather live specimens.

Aquarists should have excellent communication skills in order to write reports and interact with coworkers. They need to be in good physical shape, and hear and see well. Some employers also require a certain strength level, since aquarists have to lift equipment, feed, and the animals themselves. Aquarists may have to travel to participate in research expeditions and collect samples. As a result, they will be away from home for periods of time and work in rough conditions.

Education and Training

Most aquariums hire aquarists who have a college degree in biology with extra studies in marine and aquatic science. Volunteer work is important preparation for a career as an aquarist. Any experience you can get working directly with mammals or fish will give you an advantage over other applicants.

A penguin aquarist releases a baby penguin into an exhibit at the New England Aquarium. (Winslow Townson, AP Images)

Aquarists must be able to dive to feed fish and maintain tanks and to collect new specimens. They wear wetsuits that keep them from getting cold while working. Scuba certification, with a special rescue diver classification, is needed for this job. Employers will expect you to pass a diving physical examination before hiring you as an aquarist.

Words to Learn

aquarium a place where living aquatic plants and animals are studied and exhibited; also, a tank, bowl, or other water-filled structure in which living aquatic plants and animals are exhibited

breeding the sexual pairing of two members of the same species for the purpose of producing offspring

conservation the practice of preserving natural resources

coral reef a living structure in the ocean that is made out of the exoskeletons of a tiny organism called a coral polyp

endangered species a species having so few individual survivors that it may become extinct, or die off

specimen a small sample of a living organism or nonliving object

tidal pool a pool of seawater left on rocks near the ocean when the water (or tide) recedes; a variety of animals live in these temporary pools, including crabs, starfish, barnacles, small fish, and sea urchins

vaccination an injection using a sterile needle and syringe that protects people and animals from diseases and parasites

wetsuit a garment that protects the wearer from the harsh conditions of the ocean or other bodies of water

Earnings

Aquarists earn from $23,000 to $40,000 a year. Aquariums usually offer continuing education opportunities to help you keep up with trends and changes in the field. They also pay travel expenses for any research or collecting expeditions.

FOR MORE INFO

For information on careers in aquatic and marine science, contact the following organizations:

Alliance of Marine Mammal Parks and Aquariums
ammpa@aol.com
http://www.ammpa.org

Association of Zoos and Aquariums
8403 Colesville Road, Suite 710
Silver Spring, MD 20910-3314
301-562-0777
http://www.aza.org

Outlook

In the next decade, there will be little change in the number of job openings for aquarists. This is a popular career field, and many people want to enter it. Some zoos have begun to add aquariums to their exhibits, but the number of aquariums in the United States is still small. Aquarists with advanced education and years of experience in the field will have the strongest job prospects. Opportunities for new graduates with little experience will be best at smaller aquariums, oceanariums, and research institutes.

What Farmers Do

Farmers grow crops, such as peanuts, corn, wheat, cotton, fruits, or vegetables. They also raise cattle, pigs, sheep, chickens, and turkeys for food and keep herds of dairy cattle for milk. Throughout the early history of the United States, farming was a family affair. Today, however, family farms are disappearing. Most large farms are now run by agricultural corporations.

EXPLORING

- Learn more about different types of farming by visiting Web sites such as The Basics of Bee-keeping (http://www.hobby farms.com/crops-and-garden ing/beekeeping-14945.aspx), Dairy Farming Today (http:// www.dairyfarmingtoday.org), Organic Farming Research Foun-dation (http://ofrf.org/resources/ organicfaqs.html), U.S. Depart-ment of Agriculture (http://www. usda.gov), and What is Aquacul-ture? (http://aquaculture.noaa. gov/what/welcome.html).
- Visit farms in your community.
- Talk to a farmer about his or her career. Ask the following questions: What made you want to become a farmer? What do you like most and least about your job? How did you train to become a farmer? What advice would you give to someone who is interested in the career?

Farmers need good soil and a lot of water for their crops and animals. They need to know how to bring water to their plants and add rich nutrients to the soil. They also need to know how to keep their animals and crops healthy. They must control insects and diseases that will damage or destroy crops or livestock. They also must provide proper care, such as clean, warm shelters, proper food, and special breeding programs.

Livestock farmers buy calves (baby cows) from ranchers who breed and raise them. They feed and fatten young cattle and often raise their own corn and hay to lower feeding costs. They need to be familiar with cattle diseases and proper methods of feeding. They provide their cattle with fenced pasturage and adequate shelter from rough weather.

Sheep ranchers raise sheep primarily for their wool. Large herds are maintained on rangeland in the western states.

Dairy farmers are mostly concerned with producing high-grade milk, but they also raise corn and grain to feed their animals. Dairy animals must be milked twice each day. Farmers clean stalls and barns by washing, sweeping, and sterilizing milking equipment with boiling water.

Poultry farmers usually do not hatch their own chicks but buy them from commercial hatcheries. The primary job of poultry farmers is to keep their flocks healthy. They provide shelter from the chickens' natural enemies and from extreme weather conditions. The shelters are kept extremely clean, because diseases can spread through a flock rapidly. Some poultry farmers raise chickens to be sold for food. Others specialize in the production of eggs.

DID YOU KNOW?

- In colonial America, almost 95 percent of the population were farmers. They planted corn, wheat, flax, and tobacco. Livestock, including hogs, cattle, sheep, and goats were imported from Europe. Farmers raised hay to feed livestock and just enough other crops to supply their families with a balanced diet throughout the year.
- More than one-half of the world's population is still engaged in farming today.
- In the United States, farm employment dropped from 9.9 million in 1950 to 1.3 million in 2006.

A livestock farmer feeds one of his Texas Longhorn cattle by hand. (Steve Biehn, *The Daily Ardmoreite*/AP Images)

Beekeepers set up and manage bee hives. They harvest and sell honey. They also raise bees for lease to farmers to help pollinate their crops.

Aquaculturists raise fish, shellfish (such as crab, lobster, and shrimp), or other aquatic life (such as aquatic plants) under controlled conditions for profit and/or human consumption. They are also known as *fish farmers, fish culturists,* and *mariculturists.*

Education and Training

Courses in math and science, especially chemistry, earth science, and botany, are important. Accounting, bookkeeping, and computer courses are also very helpful.

After high school, enroll in either a two-year or a four-year course of study in a college of agriculture. For a person with no farm experience, earning a bachelor's degree in agriculture is very important.

Some universities offer advanced studies in horticulture, animal science, agronomy, and agricultural economics. Most students in agricultural colleges also take courses in farm management, business, finance, and economics.

Earnings

The amount of money a farmer makes changes from year to year depending on weather, the condition of their farm machinery, the demand for their crops and livestock, and the costs of feed, land, and equipment. For example, if weather is bad, their crops may be ruined. This will cause them to earn less money.

According to the U.S. Department of Labor, farmers and ranchers had average annual earnings of $33,360 in 2007. Earnings ranged from less than $21,230 to $80,010 or more. Most farmers, especially those running small farms, earn

Words to Learn

breeding the sexual pairing of two members of the same species for the purpose of producing offspring

conservation the practice of preserving natural resources

fertilizer natural and chemical elements that help plants to grow; chemical fertilizers can be harmful if used in too large quantities

grazing the process of eating, typically by livestock on rangeland or in farm pastures

irrigation to supply water artificially to land that is dry

organic farming a farming practice that uses environmentally friendly methods to grow plants and raise animals

overgrazing the result of livestock eating plants in a certain area for a long time—not allowing the plants to regrow

FOR MORE INFO

The federation hosts youth conferences and other events for those interested in farming.

American Farm Bureau Federation
600 Maryland Avenue, SW
Suite 1000W
Washington, DC 20024-2555
202-406-3600
http://www.fb.org

Organizations such as 4-H and the National FFA Organization offer good opportunities for learning about, visiting, and participating in farming activities.

4-H Clubs
7100 Connecticut Avenue
Chevy Chase, MD 20815
301-961-2800
info@fourhcouncil.edu
http://www.4h-usa.org

National FFA Organization
6060 FFA Drive
PO Box 68960
Indianapolis, IN 46268-0960
317-802-6060
http://www.ffa.org

For general information on agriculture, contact
U.S. Department of Agriculture
1400 Independence Avenue, SW
Washington, DC 20250-0002
202-720-2791
http://www.usda.gov

For information on aquaculture, contact
World Aquaculture Society
143 J. M. Parker Coliseum
Louisiana State University
Baton Rouge, LA 70803
225-578-3137
http://www.was.org

incomes from nonfarm activities that may be several times larger than their farm incomes.

Outlook

Because farming is such a risky business, those entering the career cannot make it without family support or financial aid. Reports show that the number of farmers or farm laborers is decreasing. Rising costs and the trend toward larger farms are forcing out small farmers. Some new jobs are opening up for *organic farmers,* those who use environmentally friendly methods to grow plants and raise animals.

Fish and Game Wardens

What Fish and Game Wardens Do

Fish and game wardens protect wildlife and manage natural resources. They also teach the public and make sure that environmental laws are followed. Fish and game wardens are also called *wildlife conservationists, wildlife inspectors, refuge rangers,* and *refuge officers.*

The conservation, or protection, of fish and wildlife is a task that grows more complex each year. Increasing pollution and changes in the environment are putting many animals at risk. To accomplish its mission, the U.S. Fish and Wildlife Service, for example, employs many of the country's best biologists, wildlife managers, engineers, and law enforcement agents. These professionals work to save endangered and threatened species and conserve migratory birds and inland fisheries. They also provide expert advice to other federal agencies, industry, and foreign governments and manage more than 700 offices and field stations. These personnel work in every state and territory—from the Arctic Ocean to the South Pacific, and from the Atlantic to the Caribbean.

Wildlife inspectors and *special agents* are two jobs that fall in the fish and game warden category of the U.S. Fish and Wildlife Service. Wildlife inspectors monitor the legal trade of federally protected fish and wildlife. They also intercept, or stop, illegal imports and exports. Some animals are so rare that it is against the law to hunt them or bring them into or take them out of the United States. At points of entry into the United States, wildlife inspectors examine shipping containers, live animals, wildlife

EXPLORING

- Learn more about endangered animals by reading books and magazines. Here are a few book suggestions: *The Atlas of Endangered Species* (University of California Press, 2008); *Endangered Animals,* by Rhonda Lucas Donald (Children's Press, 2002); and *Endangered: Wildlife on the Brink of Extinction,* by George C. McGavin (Firefly Books, 2006).

- Visit your local nature centers and park preserves often. Attend any classes or special lectures that are available. There may be opportunities to volunteer to help clean up sites, plant trees, or maintain pathways and trails.

- Get to know your local wildlife. What kind of insects, birds, fish, and other animals live in your area? Are any threatened or endangered? Visit the U.S. Fish and Wildlife Service's Web site, http://www.fws.gov, for a list.

- Interview a fish and game warden about his or her career. Ask the following questions: What made you want to enter the field? What do you like most and least about your job? How did you train to become a fish and game warden? What advice would you give to someone who is interested in the career?

products such as animal skins, and documents. Inspectors, who work closely with special agents, may seize shipments as evidence, conduct investigations, and testify in courts of law.

Special agents of the U.S. Fish and Wildlife Service are trained criminal investigators who enforce federal wildlife laws throughout the country. Special agents conduct investigations, which may include surveillance (observing people to see if they are breaking the law), undercover work, making arrests, and preparing cases for court. These agents enforce migratory bird regulations and investigate illegal trade in protected wildlife.

Refuge rangers or refuge managers work at 550 national refuges across the country. They help protect and conserve migratory and native species of birds, mammals, fish, endangered species, and other wildlife. Many of these refuges also offer outdoor recreational opportunities and educational programs.

Education and Training

Courses in biology and other sciences, geography, mathematics, social studies, and physical education will help you prepare for this career.

To become a fish and game warden you must have a bachelor's degree or three years of work experience. Higher positions require at least one year of graduate studies. Some pro-

The National Wildlife Refuge System

The National Wildlife Refuge System (http://www.fws.gov/refuges) is a system of public lands and waters set aside to conserve America's fish, wildlife, and plants. The 96 million acre system includes

- more than 700 species of birds, 250 reptile and amphibian species, 220 species of mammals, and more than 200 species of fish
- 550 national wildlife refuges
- thousands of smaller wetlands and other special management areas
- 66 national fish hatcheries
- 64 fishery resource offices
- 78 ecological services field stations

A game warden holds a set of elk antlers that are being held as evidence of poaching by the Nevada Department of Wildlife. (Debra Reid, AP Images)

fessional positions, such as biologist or manager, require master's or doctoral degrees.

On-the-job training is given for most positions. Special agents receive 18 weeks of formal training in criminal investigation and wildlife law enforcement techniques at the Federal Law Enforcement Training Center in Glynco, Georgia.

Fish and game wardens should be in good physical shape since they spend a lot of time outdoors in sometimes rugged conditions monitoring and protecting wildlife. To qualify for a special agent position, they must meet strict medical, physical, and psychological requirements. They must also participate in mandatory drug testing and psychological screening programs.

DID YOU KNOW?

Endangered species are those that have so few individual survivors that they may become extinct (die off). (A threatened species is one that is in danger of being elevated to endangered status.) At least 1,319 plants and animals in the United States alone currently are endangered, according to the U.S. Fish and Wildlife Service. Visit http://www.fws.gov/endangered to learn more about endangered species and what the U.S. Fish and Wildlife Service is doing to protect these plants and animals.

It is important to keep in mind that fish and game wardens don't just work with fish and game. They spend a lot of time working with other conservation professionals and with the general public. Therefore, they must have good communication skills and enjoy working with people as much as animals.

Earnings

In the wide variety of positions available at the U.S. Fish and Wildlife Service, salaries range from $21,000 for new workers up to $149,000 for more advanced positions. Law enforcement workers, especially special agents, receive higher salaries than support workers because their jobs are more dangerous.

FOR MORE INFO

You can learn more about fish and game wardens and related employment opportunities by contacting the following organizations:

National Park Service
U.S. Department
of the Interior
1849 C Street, NW
Washington, DC 20240-0001

202-208-6843
http://www.nps.gov

U.S. Fish and Wildlife Service
U.S. Department
of the Interior
4401 North Fairfax Drive
Arlington, VA 22203-1610
800-344-WILD
http://www.fws.gov

Outlook

There will always be a need for fish and game wardens to protect natural resources. The largest number of jobs in the field are with the U.S. Fish and Wildlife Service and the National Park Service. State agencies, such as departments of natural resources or departments of parks and recreation, also offer jobs.

Employment growth in this field depends on politics and government. Some presidents and governors spend more on wildlife concerns, while others make cutbacks in this area. If less money is spent on wildlife, than there will be fewer jobs for fish and game wardens. When funding is available, there are more opportunities for fish and game wardens. When funding is cut, fish and game warden positions may be eliminated or agencies may hire fewer workers.

Horse Grooms

What Horse Grooms Do

Horses are valued for their speed, grace, and beauty. They are bred and raced at stables and racetracks all over the country. Owners and trainers invest a great deal of time and effort to make sure their horses are well cared for. *Horse grooms* are an important part of the team they hire to do this. Horse grooms also work for individuals or riding stables that need help grooming their horses.

Grooms have many daily duties. They must feed and water each horse under their care. Depending on its size and age, a

EXPLORING

- Visit the following Web sites to learn more about horses, horse care, and horseback riding: American Quarter Horse Youth Association (http://www.aqha.com/youth), Certified Horsemanship Association (http://www.cha-ahse.org), and Junior Master Horseman (http://www.juniormaster-horseman.com).
- Take riding lessons.
- Spend time at stables to watch and learn about the care of horses. You may be able to volunteer or work part-time as a stable helper. This type of work is not always pleasant. You will probably have to shovel manure and clean stables—but you will learn a lot from being around horses and their grooms.
- Talk to a horse groom about his or her career.

DID YOU KNOW?

- Horses are herbivores, meaning that they only eat plants.
- There are approximately 400 different breeds of horses.
- Horses weigh anywhere from 120 to 2,200 pounds.
- Horses live an average of 20-25 years. The oldest horses can live to 50 or 60 years of age.
- The average height (measured at the shoulders) of horses ranges from 2½ feet to nearly six feet.
- There are approximately 33,000 wild horses and burros living in 10 Western U.S. states.

Sources: *National Geographic*, Bureau of Land Management

horse can eat as much as 20 pounds of hay and 12 pounds of grain a day, and drink more than 12 gallons of water. Horses also need some salt every day. Many take extra protein, vitamins, and minerals to balance their diets. Grooms prepare the feed and make sure each horse gets what it needs to stay healthy. This is especially important for racing horses, who must be in top shape.

Horses also must get a certain amount of exercise—at least an hour per day. Other track workers—specially trained *exercisers*—are responsible for this. After exercise or a race, workers called *hotwalkers* walk a horse until it cools down.

The groom then bathes, brushes, and combs the horse to keep its coat healthy and help improve muscle tone. The groom uses a variety of tools for this job. Curry combs, dandy brushes, and body brushes help loosen dirt and dead hair, cleaning the horse's coat. A special comb may be used for its mane and tail. A hoof pick is used to clean the bottom of its feet. Grooms help groom horses, but they are not responsible for maintaining horseshoes. This is the work of a trained technician called a *farrier*.

Grooms are important to the running of a stable or racetrack. Because they spend so much time with the horses, grooms often are the first to recognize when something is wrong. They notice when a horse stops eating properly, or "goes off its feed." They notice when a horse is lame and may have been injured during regular exercise or a race. Finding these problems early is very important, both for the horse's health and for its ability to race.

A groom cares for a racehorse. (Al Behrman, AP Images)

To be a successful horse groom, you should be a strong team player, have excellent knowledge of horses and their care, be organized, be able to follow instructions, and be willing to perform

Classic Horse Tales

The beauty and power of horses have captured the imagination of storytellers for centuries. Here are some classic tales to read:

Black Beauty, by Anna Sewell
The Black Stallion, by Walter Farley
Man O'War, by Walter Farley
Misty of Chincoteague, by Marguerite Henry
My Friend Flicka, by Mary O'Hara

sometimes repetitious and physically demanding tasks.

Education and Training

A high school education is helpful for horse groom careers, but not required. Trainers prefer to hire grooms who know a little about biology (the study of living organisms) or physiology (the study of the functions of living organisms). Biology and physiology are important because grooms must know how to tell when their horses are suffering physical problems, and when they need medical attention.

Earnings

Horse grooms are paid based on how many horses they take care of, so their wages vary. An average groom is responsible for four to five horses. Most grooms are paid at least $75-$100 per week per horse, but there is no minimum wage.

Full-time horse grooms who work at race tracks often live in quarters on site. Grooms sometimes are "staked," or offered a percentage of their horses' winnings, since successful racing depends a great deal on how well cared for the horses are. Grooms who work with racing horses travel to different race tracks with the trainer and the rest of the team involved in getting the horse ready for a race.

Outlook

Employment in this field should grow about as fast as the average for other careers over the next few years. Horses require

FOR MORE INFO

For information on the horse industry, contact

American Horse Council
1616 H Street, NW, 7th Floor
Washington, DC 20006-4918
202-296-4031
AHC@horsecouncil.org
http://www.horsecouncil.org

For information on membership and to read free resources, such as Basic Horse Care and Horse Career Possibilities, visit the council's Web site.

American Youth Horse Council
6660 #D-451 Delmonico
Colorado Springs, CO 80919
http://www.ayhc.com

You can find out more about horse racing from this organization. Its Web site also has links to many other organizations for people who are interested in horses.

Thoroughbred Owners and Breeders Association
PO Box 910668
Lexington, KY 40591-0668
888-606-TOBA
toba@toba.org
http://www.toba.org

For information on thoroughbred racing, contact

National Thoroughbred Racing Association
2525 Harrodsburg Road, Suite 400
Lexington, KY 40504-3359
859-245-6872
ntra@ntra.com
http://www.ntra.com

daily attention—feeding, bathing, and brushing—and stalls must be kept clean. These basic needs are the job of the groom, and must be done whether the horse is racing or not. Owners and breeders will continue to require the help of good grooms. There will also be continued demand for horse grooms who work for riding stables, farms, private owners, and any organization that has horses.

Marine Biologists

What Marine Biologists Do

Marine biologists are a special type of oceanographers. They study the plants and animals that live in oceans. Marine biologists learn about the tens of thousands of different species that live in salt water.

Marine biologists take sea voyages to study plants and animals in their natural environment. When they reach their destination, perhaps near a coral reef or other habitat, the scientists dive into the water to collect samples.

Because of the cold temperatures below the surface of the sea, marine biologists must wear wetsuits to keep warm. They use scuba gear to help them breathe under water. They may carry a tool, called a slurp gun, which can suck a fish into a specimen bag without hurting it. While underwater, biologists must watch out for dangerous fish and mammals such as sharks or stingrays. They take great care not to damage the marine environment.

Marine biologists also gather specimens from tidal pools along the shore. They may collect samples at the same time of day for days at a time. They keep samples from different pools separate and carefully write down the pool's location, the types of specimens taken, and their measurements. It is important to keep accurate records.

After they collect specimens, scientists keep them in a special portable aquarium tank on the ship. After returning to land, sometimes weeks or months later, marine biologists study the specimens in their laboratories. They might check the amount

EXPLORING

- Visit Web sites that focus on oceanography. Interesting sites include Careers in Oceanography, Marine Science, and Marine Biology (http://ocean. peterbrueggeman.com/career. html), MarineBio (http://www. marinebio.com), and Sea Grant Marine Careers (http://www. marinecareers.net).
- Read books about oceans, marine biology, animals, and careers in the field. Here are a few suggestions: *National Geographic Encyclopedia of Animals,* by Karen McGhee and George McKay (National Geographic Children's Books, 2006); *Oceans,* by Beverly McMillan and John A. Musick (Simon & Schuster Children's Publishing,

2007); *Opportunities in Marine Science and Maritime Careers,* by William Ray Heitzmann (McGraw-Hill, 2006); and *You Can Be a Woman Marine Biologist,* by Florence McAlary and Judith Love Cohen (Cascade Pass Inc., 2002).
- Visit your local aquarium to learn about marine life and about the life of a marine biologist.
- If you live near an ocean you can collect shells and other specimens. Keep a notebook to record details about what you find and where.
- Take up hobbies, such as swimming, boating, snorkeling, or fishing.
- Turtles and fish make good pets for future marine biologists.

of oxygen in a sea turtle's blood stream to learn how the turtles can stay underwater for so long. Or they might measure the blood chemistry of an arctic fish to discover how it can survive very cold temperatures.

Marine biologists study changing conditions of the ocean, such as temperature or chemicals that have polluted the water. They try to see how those changes affect the plants and animals that live there. If certain species become extinct (die off) or are no longer safe to eat, the world's food supply grows smaller.

The work of these scientists is also important for improving and managing sport and commercial fishing. Through underwater exploration, these scientists have discovered that the world's coral reefs are being destroyed by humans. They have

Words to Learn

coral reef a living structure in the ocean that is made out of the exoskeletons of a tiny organism called a coral polyp

community a group of organisms that share a particular habitat

ecosystem a group of organisms living together with nonliving components

habitat an area where an organism or group of organisms normally lives

global warming the slow rise in our planet's average temperature caused by an increase in greenhouse gases (such as carbon dioxide, methane, and nitrous oxide)

inventory of species counting the number of different types of plants or animals in a given area

migration the mass movement of a group of organisms during which normal behaviors such as breeding are ignored; migration often occurs as a result of the changing of the seasons

specimen a small sample of a living organism or nonliving object

tidal pool a pool of seawater left on rocks near the ocean shore when the water (or tide) recedes; a variety of animals live in these temporary pools, including crabs, starfish, barnacles, small fish, and sea urchins

wetsuit a garment that protects the wearer from the harsh conditions of the ocean or other bodies of water

DID YOU KNOW?

- Coral reefs make up less than .02 percent of the ocean's bottom, but contain more than 25 percent of all life in the sea.
- Most coral reefs are found in water that has a temperature of 61 to 86 degrees Fahrenheit.
- There are three types of coral reefs. Barrier reefs are found far out in the ocean and are not connected to the mainland. Fringing reefs are connected to the mainland. Atolls are islands that are made of coral. They surround a lagoon.
- Approximately 10 percent of coral reefs have been destroyed and about 60 percent are in danger of being killed.
- Human development, global warming, pollution, and hurricanes are the biggest threats to coral reefs.

Source: Exploring the Environment: Coral Reefs (http://www.cotf.edu/ete/modules/coralreef/CRmain.html)

also charted the migration of whales and counted the decreasing numbers of certain species. They have seen dolphins being caught by accident in tuna fishermen's nets. By telling people about their discoveries through written reports and research papers, marine biologists help people and governments make changes that protect the environment.

Education and Training

If you want to be a marine biologist, you should like math and science. Biology, botany, and chemistry classes are important to take in high school. Although you can get a job as a marine biologist with a bachelor's degree, most marine biologists have a master's or doctoral degree.

Earnings

Salaries vary depending on how much education and experience you have. The average wildlife biologist earns about $55,000

FOR MORE INFO

For information on careers and marine science, contact the following organizations:

American Institute of Biological Sciences
1444 I Street, NW, Suite 200
Washington, DC 20005-6535
202-628-1500
http://www.aibs.org

American Society of Limnology and Oceanography
5400 Bosque Boulevard,
Suite 680
Waco, TX 76710-4446
800-929-2756
http://www.aslo.org

For ocean news, contact
The Oceanography Society
PO Box 1931
Rockville, MD 20849-1931
301-251-7708
info@tos.org
http://www.tos.org

For information on diving instruction and certification, contact
PADI
30151 Tomas Street
Rancho Santa Margarita, CA 92688
800-729-7234
http://www.padi.com

yearly. Those who have doctorates in marine biology can earn as much as $80,000 a year. Senior scientists or full professors at universities can earn more than $100,000 a year.

Outlook

Many people want to work as marine biologists—especially in top positions. Opportunities in research are especially hard to find. Those who have advanced degrees and specialized knowledge in math and computer science will have the best chances for employment. Changes in the earth's environment, such as global warming, will require more research and so create more jobs. Marine biologists should be able to find jobs managing the world's fisheries, making medicines from marine organisms, and cultivating (growing) marine food alternatives, such as seaweed and plankton.

Naturalists

What Naturalists Do

Naturalists study the natural world. They do so in order to learn the best way to preserve the earth and its living creatures—humans, animals, and plants. They teach the public about the environment. They show people what they can do about such

EXPLORING

- Read books and magazines about plants and animals and a career as a naturalist.
- Visit the following Web sites to learn more about animals: Animal Diversity Web (http://animaldiversity.ummz.umich.edu), Animal Fact Guide (http://www.animalfactguide.com), and Yahoo!: Kids: Animals (http://kids.yahoo.com/animals).
- Visit your local nature centers and park preserves often. Attend any classes or special lectures they offer. There may be opportunities to volunteer to help clean up sites, plant trees, or maintain pathways and trails.
- Hiking, animal watching, and photography are good hobbies for future naturalists.
- Keep a journal that details all the plants and animals you see in your neighborhood.
- Get to know your local wildlife. What kind of insects, birds, fish, mammals, and other animals live in your area? Your librarian will be able to help you find books that identify local flora and fauna.
- Talk to a naturalist about his or her job.

hazards as pollution. Pollution can cause humans, animals, and plants to get sick or even die.

Naturalists also can work as *nature resource managers, wildlife conservationists, ecologists,* and *environmental educators* for many different employers.

Depending on where they work, naturalists may protect and conserve wildlife or particular kinds of land, such as prairie or wetlands. Other naturalists research and carry out plans to restore lands that have been damaged by erosion, fire, or development. Some naturalists recreate wildlife habitats and nature trails. They plant trees, for example, or label existing plants (so

The Beginnings of Conservation

During the 19th century in the United States, many great forests were cut down and huge areas of land were leveled for open-pit mining and quarrying. More disease occurred with the increase of air pollution from the smokestacks of factories, home chimneys, and engine exhaust. At the same time there was a dramatic decrease in populations of elk, antelope, deer, bison, and other animals of the Great Plains (a geographic area of North America that includes parts of 10 U.S. states and three Canadian provinces). Some types of bear, cougar, and wolf became extinct, as well as several kinds of birds, such as the passenger pigeon. In the latter half of the 19th century, the government set up a commission to develop scientific management of fisheries. It established the first national park (Yellowstone National Park in Wyoming, Idaho, and Montana), and set aside the first forest reserves. These early steps led to the modern conservation movement.

hikers and campers know what they are). *Fish and wildlife wardens* help manage populations of fish, hunted animals, and protected animals. They control hunting and fishing and make sure species are thriving but not overpopulating their territories. *Wildlife managers, range managers,* and *conservationists* also maintain the plant and animal life in a certain area. They work in parks or on ranges that have both domestic livestock (animals such as cattle that have been tamed by humans) and wild animals (such as deer, bears, and coyotes). They test soil and water for pollution and nutrients. They count plant and animal populations each season.

DID YOU KNOW?

Where Naturalists Work

- Wildlife museums
- Private nature centers
- Large zoos
- Parks and nature preserves
- Arboretums
- Botanical gardens
- Government agencies such as the U.S. Fish and Wildlife Service or the National Park Service

Naturalists also work indoors. They raise money for projects, write reports, keep detailed records, and write articles, brochures, and newsletters to tell the public about their work. They might campaign for support for protection of an endangered species by holding meetings and hearings. Other public education activities include leading tours and nature walks and holding demonstrations, exhibits, and classes.

Naturalists should enjoy working outdoors since they spend the majority of their time outside in all kinds of weather. They should also be able to work well with other environmental professionals and the general public. They should be good teachers in order to educate the public about nature and environmental issues. Finally, naturalists should have good writing skills. They need these to prepare educational materials and grant proposals.

Education and Training

If you are interested in this field, you should take basic science courses in high school, including biology, chemistry, and earth science. Botany courses and clubs are also helpful, since they will give you direct experience observing plant growth and health.

Naturalists must have at least a bachelor's degree in biology, zoology, chemistry, botany, natural history, or environmental science. A master's degree is not required, but is helpful. Many naturalists have a master's degree in education. Experience gained through summer jobs and volunteer work can be just as important as educational requirements. Experience working with the public is also helpful.

Earnings

Starting salaries for full-time naturalists range from about $20,000 to $29,000 per year. Some part-time workers, however, earn as little as minimum wage ($7.25 per hour). For some positions, housing and vehicles may be provided. Earnings vary for

FOR MORE INFO

For information on careers, contact
American Society of Naturalists
http://www.amnat.org

For information about career opportunities, contact
Bureau of Land Management
U.S. Department of the Interior
1849 C Street
Washington, DC 20240-0001
http://www.blm.gov

For information on conservation programs, contact
National Wildlife Federation
11100 Wildlife Center Drive
Reston, VA 20190-5362
800-822-9919
http://www.nwf.org

For information on conservation and volunteer opportunities, contact
Student Conservation Association
689 River Road
PO Box 550
Charlestown, NH 03603-0550
603-543-1700
ask-us@thesca.org
http://www.thesca.org

For information on careers, contact
U.S. Fish and Wildlife Service
U.S. Department of the Interior
4401 North Fairfax Drive
Arlington, VA 22203-1610
http://www.fws.gov/jobs

those with more job duties or advanced degrees. The U.S. Department of Labor reports that conservation scientists (a career category that includes naturalists) earned an average annual salary of $58,720 in 2008. Conservation scientists employed by the federal government earned mean annual salaries of $69,090, and those employed by social advocacy organizations earned $54,540. Conservation scientists employed at colleges and universities earned $54,620. Experienced naturalists made $82,080 or more.

Outlook

In the next decade, the job outlook for naturalists is expected to be only fair, despite the public's increasing interest in the environment. Private nature centers and preserves—where forests, wetlands, and prairies are restored—are continuing to open in the United States. But possible government cutbacks in the amount of money provided to nature programs may limit their growth. Many people want to enter this field, which will make it difficult to land a job.

Park Rangers

What Park Rangers Do

Park rangers protect animals and preserve forests, ponds, and other natural resources. They teach visitors about parks by giving lectures and tours. They also make sure rules and regulations are followed to maintain a safe environment for visitors and wildlife. For example, they make sure that visitors

EXPLORING

- Read as much as you can about local, state, and national parks. The National Park Service's Web site, http://www.nps.gov, is a great place to start.
- Get to know your local wildlife. What kind of insects, mammals, birds, fish, and other animals live in your area? Your science teacher or librarian will be able to help you find books and Web sites that identify local flora and fauna.
- Hands-on experience can be a great advantage if you are interested in entering this competitive field. You can get this experience by getting involved in the Volunteers-in-Parks (VIP) program, which is sponsored by the National Park Service. For more information, visit http://www.nps.gov/volunteer.
- You also may be able to volunteer at state, county, or local parks. Universities and conservation organizations often have volunteer groups that work on research activities, studies, and rehabilitation efforts.

do not get too close to bears or herds of buffalo. These animals can be very dangerous and injure and even kill unsuspecting tourists. They also police the park to ensure that people are not driving motorized vehicles in areas where their presence could damage plants or wildlife or otherwise break park regulations. The National Park Service is one of the major employers of park rangers. In addition, park rangers work for other federal land and resource management agencies and similar state and local agencies.

Safety is a key responsibility for park rangers. They often require visitors to register at park offices so they will know when the visitors are expected to return from a hike or other activity. Rangers know first aid and, if there is an accident or animal attack, they may have to help visitors who have been hurt. Rangers carefully mark hiking trails and other areas to reduce the risk of injuries for visitors and to protect plants and animals.

Rangers help visitors enjoy and learn about parks. They give lectures and provide guided tours of the park, explaining why certain plants and animals live there. They might explain how and why wolves were reintroduced into Yellowstone National Park. Others may talk about efforts to protect the piping plover, a small bird that nests along beaches.

Research and conservation efforts are also a big part of a park ranger's responsibilities. They study wildlife behav-

Tips for Success

To be a successful park ranger, you should

- know how to protect plants and animals
- be a good teacher
- enjoy working outdoors
- have a pleasant personality
- be able to work with many different kinds of people
- be in good physical shape
- be able to enforce park rules and regulations
- be willing to travel to take on new assignments

ior by tagging and following certain animals. (Tagging involves placing an electronic collar or tracking device on an animal.) They may investigate sources of pollution that come from outside the park. Then they develop plans to help reduce pollution to make the park a better place for plants, animals, and visitors.

Rangers also do bookkeeping and other paperwork. They issue permits to visitors and keep track of how many people use the park. They also plan recreational activities and decide how to spend the money budgeted to the park.

Education and Training

In high school, take courses in earth science, biology, mathematics, history, English, and speech. Any classes or activities that deal with plant and animal life, the weather, geography, and interacting with others will be helpful.

Park rangers usually have bachelor's degrees in natural resource, wildlife, or recreational resource management. A degree in many other fields, such as biology or ecology, is also acceptable. Classes in forestry, geology, outdoor management, history, geography, behavioral sciences, and botany are helpful. Without a degree, you need at least three years of experience working in parks or conservation. Rangers also receive on-the-job training.

Earnings

In 2009, new rangers in the National Park Service earned between $27,026 and $35,135 annually. Rangers with some experience earned between $33,477 and $43,521. The most experienced rangers who supervise other workers earn more than

$90,000 a year. The government may provide housing to rangers who work in remote areas.

Rangers in state parks work for the state government. Rangers employed by state parks earn average starting salaries of about $25,000.

Outlook

Many people want to become park rangers. In fact, there are not enough jobs for everyone who wants to enter the field. Park ranger jobs should continue to be popular in the future. Because of this stiff competition for positions, the job outlook is

FOR MORE INFO

For information about state parks and employment opportunities, contact
National Association of State Park Directors
8829 Woodyhill Road
Raleigh, NC 27613-1134
919-676-8365
NASPD@nc.rr.com
http://www.naspd.org

For general career information, contact the following organizations:
National Parks Conservation Association
1300 19th Street, NW, Suite 300
Washington, DC 20036-1628
800-628-7275
npca@npca.org
http://www.npca.org

National Recreation and Park Association
22377 Belmont Ridge Road
Ashburn, VA 20148-4150
800-626-6772

info@nrpa.org
http://www.nrpa.org

For detailed information about careers with the National Park Service, contact
National Park Service
U.S. Department of the Interior
1849 C Street, NW
Washington, DC 20240-0001
202-208-6843
http://www.nps.gov

Contact this organization for information on volunteer positions in natural resource management for high school students.
Student Conservation Association
689 River Road
PO Box 550
Charlestown, NH 03603-0550
603-543-1700
ask-us@thesca.org
http://www.thesca.org

expected to change little. As a result, those interested in the field should attain the greatest number and widest variety of skills possible. They may wish to study subjects they can use in other fields, such as forestry, land management, conservation, wildlife management, history, and natural sciences.

Employment opportunities will be better at state and local parks—although these parks pay lower salaries than those offered by the National Park Service. Many park rangers start out as seasonal or part-time employees. This gives them a chance to break into the field and show their employers that they are good workers. In time, many part-time park rangers can transition to full-time positions. Aspiring park rangers must be willing to travel to find jobs in the field. A position as a ranger with the National Park Service may not be available in one's own state or region, but at a park that is located across the country. The same is true for positions at the state level.

Pet Groomers

What Pet Groomers Do

Pet groomers bathe, trim, shape, brush, and comb animals' coats to make them look good and help them stay healthy. They also clip nails, clean ears, and examine animals for fleas, ticks, and other health problems. Most of a pet groomer's business comes from shaggy, long-haired dogs and dogs with special grooming styles, such as poodles, schnauzers, cocker spaniels, and terriers. Show dogs—dogs that are shown in competition—are groomed frequently.

More and more cats, especially longhaired breeds, are now being taken to pet groomers. The grooming method for dogs

EXPLORING

- Take care of your family pet, including walking, feeding, and grooming.
- Offer to help your friends and neighbors take care of their pets.
- Youth organizations such as the Boy Scouts, Girl Scouts, and 4-H Clubs sponsor projects that give you opportunities to raise and care for animals.

- Volunteer to care for animals at an animal hospital, kennel, pet shop, animal shelter, nature center, or zoo.
- Learn about different breeds of dogs and cats and their special grooming needs.
- Talk to a pet groomer about his or her career.

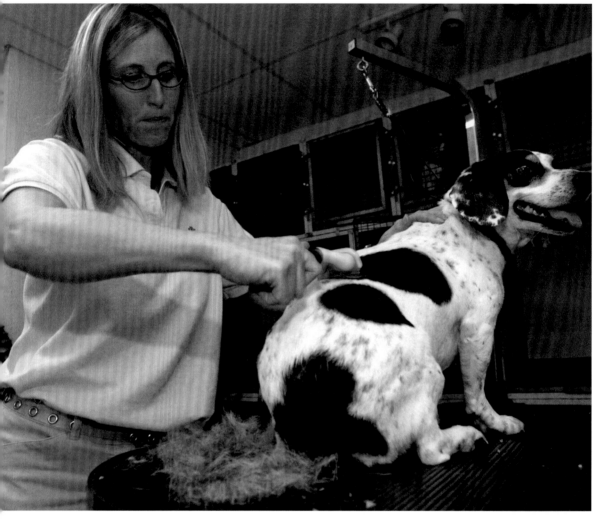

A groomer uses a grooming tool to remove hair from a dog. (Tom Gannam, AP Images)

and cats is essentially the same, although cats do not receive the full bathing treatment given to dogs. Pet groomers first place the animal on a grooming table and steady it with a nylon collar. Some animals are extremely nervous and uncooperative during grooming procedures. If the groomer is unable to calm the animal and gain its trust, he or she may muzzle it (cover its mouth). Some pets even have to be tranquilized (calmed or put to sleep by medication) by a veterinarian for the grooming procedure.

Groomers brush the animals to remove shedding hair and dead skin. The brushing is followed by cutting and shaping, when necessary. The groomer then cleans the animal's ears and trims its nails, taking care not to cut them too short, which is painful and causes bleeding. In the case of dogs, bathing follows. The dog is lowered into a stainless steel tub. Then it is sprayed with warm water, scrubbed with a special shampoo, and rinsed. At this point, any special treatments, such as deodorizing or treating ticks or fleas, are completed. Most dogs can be groomed in about 90 minutes. Poodles usually take the longest because of their intricate clipping pattern. Also, shaggier breeds whose coats are badly matted and overgrown can take several hours. Most cats can be groomed in much less time.

Pet groomers are employed by grooming salons, kennels, pet shops, veterinary practices, animal hospitals, and grooming schools. Many pet groomers choose to go into business for themselves because they enjoy being their own boss and setting their own hours. Self-employed workers also often have higher earnings than those who are not self employed.

Magazines for Groomers

Groomer to Groomer
http://www.groomertogroomer.com

GroomingBusiness
http://www.groomingbusiness.com

Pet Age
http://www.petage.com

Education and Training

There are three basic ways to become a dog groomer. Many groomers teach themselves by reading books on the subject and then practicing on their own and friends' pets. They learn

Tips for Success

To be a successful pet groomer, you should

- love animals
- be very knowledgeable about pet grooming
- have patience
- not be afraid of animals
- be in good physical shape
- have excellent business skills (if running your own business)
- enjoy working with your hands
- have good eyesight
- have good manual dexterity

the more complicated cuts and important safety precautions while working for an experienced groomer. Some groomers begin by working in a veterinarian's office, kennel, or pet shop, and learn on the job They may begin with shampooing animals and work up to brushing, clipping, and expert trimming. Other groomers enroll in accredited pet grooming schools. At these schools, they study bathing, brushing, clipping, the care of the ears and nails, coat and skin conditions, animal anatomy terminology, and sanitation.

Many high school courses are useful to those interested in pet grooming, such as anatomy and physiology (the study of the structure and functions of living organisms), health, science, first aid, business math, English, and psychology. A high school diploma is not required to become a pet groomer, but it is helpful for advancement.

Earnings

Groomers who work for a salon or another groomer usually keep 50 to 60 percent of the fees they charge. The U.S. Department of Labor reports that average earnings of nonfarm animal caretakers (the category in which pet groomers are classified) were $18,890 in 2007. Those just starting out in the field earned less than $14,000. Groomers with a lot of experience and many clients earned $31,000 or more. Those who own and operate their own grooming services can earn higher

FOR MORE INFO

For more information about grooming and related professions, including grooming competitions and conferences, contact
Intergroom
76 Carol Drive
Dedham, MA 02026-6635
781-326-3376
http://www.intergroom.com

This association offers membership options for dog groomers and other canine care professionals.
International Association of Canine Professionals
http://www.dogpro.org

For industry information, contact
International Society of Canine Cosmetologists

2702 Covington Drive
Garland, TX 75040-3822
http://www.petstylist.com

For information on shows, new grooming products and techniques, and workshops, contact
National Dog Groomers Association of America
PO Box 101
Clark, PA 16113-0101
724-962-2711
http://www.nationaldoggroomers.com

For industry information, contact
Pet Care Services Association
1702 East Pikes Peak Avenue
Colorado Springs, CO 80909-5717
877-570-7788
http://www.petcareservices.org

salaries. Groomers usually buy their own clipping equipment, including barber's shears, brushes, and clippers.

Outlook

Employment for groomers should be very good during the next decade. Each year, more people are keeping dogs and cats as pets, and they are spending more money to pamper them. There will also be opportunities for groomers who are prepared to groom the growing number of nontraditional pets, such as ferrets, birds, and reptiles.

Pet Shop Workers

What Do Pet Shop Workers Do

It's a lot of fun to visit a pet shop. There are birds chirping in their cages. Dogs barking. There are also furry animals such as hamsters and guinea pigs and all kinds of multi-colored fish swimming in their tanks. There might even be turtles, lizards, and frogs. But a pet store is not all fun and games. It takes dedicated workers to run a pet shop.

Pet shop workers are involved in the daily upkeep of a pet store. They sell pets and pet supplies, including food, medicine,

EXPLORING

- Read books and visit Web sites about pet care. Interesting Web sites include Animaland (http://www2.aspca.org/site/PageServer?pagename=kids_home), Care for Animals (http://www.avma.org/careforanimals/default.asp), Kids: Pet Care (http://www.spca.bc.ca/kids/animalcare), Petpourri (http://www.avma.org/careforanimals/kidscorner), and zootoo (http://www.zootoo.com).

- Learn more about pet care by getting your own pet. Ask your parents first for permission.
- Volunteer at animal shelters, zoos, and other animal care facilities to get experience working with animals.
- Join agricultural clubs and 4-H clubs to learn about animal care and responsibilities.
- Talk to a pet store worker about his or her career.

toys, carriers, and educational books and DVDs. They answer customers' questions and offer animal care advice. They keep the store, aquariums, and animal cages clean and look after the health of the pets for sale. They also stock shelves, order products from distributors, and keep records on the animals and products they sell.

Pet shops employ the same kinds of workers that are found in any retail store. These include cashiers, managers, stock workers, bookkeepers, and sales and marketing workers. Pet shop owners may also hire pet groomers, animal caretakers, and animal trainers. A pet shop must have a staff that loves animals, knows a lot about pets and their care, and is good with customers.

DID YOU KNOW?

The most popular exotic pets in the United States in 2007 were:

1. Fish
2. Rabbits
3. Turtles
4. Hamsters
5. Livestock
6. Lizards
7. Guinea pigs
8. Ferrets
9. Birds
10. Other rodents
11. Snakes
12. Gerbils
13. Other reptiles

Source: *U.S. Pet Ownership & Demographics Sourcebook*

The most important jobs for pet shop workers are animal care and customer service. Most pet shop workers help prepare the store for opening. They make sure the shop is clean, the shelves are in order, the aisles are clear, and the cash register is ready for sales. They clean cages and fish tanks and make sure the animals are fed and watered. Though some pet shops continue to sell dogs and cats, most buyers for those kinds of animals purchase directly from breeders, or select animals from shelters and the humane societies. Today's pet shops generally specialize in birds, fish, and small animals such as hamsters and mice.

Pet shop workers also wait on customers. Customers ask pet shop workers for advice on caring for their pets. They expect them to know everything about the pets they are selling. They also ask them about pet food, medicines, and other supplies.

Pet shops may offer a variety of services, including pet grooming, dog training, and animal boarding. They may also offer animal vaccinations.

Education and Training

Math courses will teach you the skills you need for figuring proper feed and medication amounts for the animals. A knowledge of chemistry will come in handy when preparing medications and chemicals for the aquariums. Biology will introduce you to the body structure and functions of various kinds of animals.

You can easily get a job at a pet store without any college education or special training. Pet shops often hire high school students for part-time and summer jobs. Store owners usually hire someone with a love of animals and some knowledge of animal care for entry-level positions such as clerk, cashier, and sales worker. For management positions, a pet shop owner may want someone with more education and experience. They might want someone who has an associate's or bachelor's degree in business or retail management.

Earnings

Entry-level pet shop workers earn minimum wage, and even experienced employees probably won't make much more than that. The average store manager makes less than $30,000 a year. Managers at large pet store chains such as PETCO and PetSmart earn higher salaries.

Tips for Success

To be a successful pet shop worker, you should

- know a lot about animals
- be friendly and outgoing
- enjoy answering questions about pets and pet care
- be able to deal with sometimes difficult customers
- be detail oriented
- be on time
- have good math skills
- not mind getting your hands dirty sometimes

FOR MORE INFO

For more information on the pet products industry, contact
American Pet Products Association
255 Glenville Road
Greenwich, CT 06831-4148
203-532-0000
http://www.appma.org

For information on retail careers, visit the federation's Web site.
National Retail Federation
325 7th Street, NW, Suite 1100
Washington, DC 20004-2818
800-NRF-HOW2
http://www.nrf.com

Outlook

Americans spend more than $45 billion each year on their pets. They spend a good portion of this amount at pet stores. The amount we spend on pet care increases each year. This suggests that there will be good job prospects for those who work in pet stores. Workers at large pet chains will have the best employment opportunities. But small stores will survive because customers like a more friendly, personalized buying experience that these stores offer.

Pet Sitters

What Pet Sitters Do

Pet sitters visit clients' homes to care for their pets. During short, daily visits, pet sitters feed the animals, give them fresh water, and play with them. They also clean up after them, give them medications when needed, and let them in and out of the house for exercise. *Dog walkers* may be responsible only for taking their customers' dogs out for exercise. Pet sitters may also offer overnight services to look after the clients' houses as well as their pets.

Pet sitters let themselves into clients' homes with their own sets of keys and care for the animals while their owners are at work or out of town. They play with and sometimes feed the ani-

EXPLORING

- Read books, newsletters, and magazines about pet care.
- Offer pet sitting services to neighbors or friends. Start with one or two clients. If you do a good job, they will recommend you to other friends and neighbors. You will get valuable experience taking care of animals, and you will also learn about running a business.

- Talk to a pet sitter about his or her career. Ask the following questions: What made you want to become a pet sitter? What do you like most and least about your job? How did you train to become a pet sitter? What advice would you give to someone who is interested in the career?

mals and provide care, attention, and affection at times when the owners cannot. Pet sitters must do some "dirty work," such as cleaning litter boxes and any messes that the animals make. Some pet sitters offer services that may include taking a pet to the vet, grooming the pet, or providing advice (known as consulting).

Pet sitters usually visit clients' homes one to three times per day. Each visit lasts 30 to 60 minutes. Often, pet sitters are responsible for other tasks, such as bringing in the mail and newspapers, watering plants, and making sure the house is securely locked when they leave.

Most pet sitters work alone, without coworkers or employees. In addition to caring for animals, pet sitters have to manage their businesses. They have to find new clients, schedule appointments, and give referrals for boarders and vets. Pet sitters also must work weekends and holidays, since pet owners are often away from home during this time.

To be a successful pet sitter, you must love animals and be comfortable around them. You should also be self-motivated and a hard worker in order to keep your business running successfully and have excellent communication skills in order to interact well with customers and attract new business. Another key skill for pet sitters is being trustworthy since you will be working in clients' homes and trusted with the care of their pets. You should also be organized and prepared for emergency situations.

DID YOU KNOW?

Pet Ownership in the United States, 2007

Type of Pet	Percentage of U.S. Households Owning Pet
Dogs	37.2 percent
Cats	32.4 percent
Birds	3.9 percent
Horses	1.8 percent

Source: U.S. Pet Ownership & Demographics Sourcebook

Education and Training

There are no special education requirements for pet sitting work. Classes in biology, health, accounting, and marketing

Get the Facts

Here are some things pet sitters need to find out from their clients in order to give the best service:

- Important routines in the pet's day—eating, sleeping, walking, or playing
- Major and minor health problems the pet may have
- Detailed information on any medication that is being given to the pet
- Whom to contact in an emergency, including names and numbers of the pet's veterinarian and veterinary hospital
- Where favorite toys are kept
- The location of the pet's favorite hiding places
- Any unusual habits the pet may have (such as changes in bowel movements, eating habits, fears, etc.)
- Where to find written verification of up-to-date vaccinations for the pet (tags on collars are good)

Source: National Association of Professional Pet Sitters

will be helpful. For this work, experience is the best education. To get experience, volunteer your pet sitting services to your neighbors or call an experienced pet sitter and ask if you can tag along or even work for a day or two. This is an excellent way to learn firsthand the duties of a pet sitter.

Pet sitters often take home study courses in animal nutrition, office procedures, and management.

Earnings

Pet sitters set their own prices and may charge by the visit, the hour, or the week. They may also charge consultation fees and extra fees on holidays. Generally, pet sitters charge between $8 and $15 a visit. A few very successful pet sitters earn more than $100,000 per year, while others make only $5,000 a year. Bigger cities offer more clients for pet sitters. Pet sitters usually make

FOR MORE INFO

For information about pet care, contact
American Society for the
Prevention of Cruelty to Animals
424 East 92nd Street
New York, NY 10128-6804
212-876-7700
http://www.aspca.org

The association offers membership options for dog walkers and other canine care professionals.
International Association of Canine Professionals
http://www.dogpro.org

For information on pet setting, contact
National Association of

Professional Pet Sitters
15000 Commerce Parkway,
Suite C
Mt. Laurel, NJ 08054-2212
856-439-0324
napps@ahint.com
http://www.petsitters.org

For career and small business information as well as general information about pet sitting, contact
Pet Sitters International
201 East King Street
King, NC 27021-9161
336-983-9222
info@petsit.com
http://www.petsit.com

around $10,000-$15,000 a year in their first five years. After eight years or more they may earn around $40,000 a year.

Outlook

Pet sitting businesses are expected to grow rapidly in the next few years. Many pet owners like to use in-home pet sitters instead of boarders and kennels because their pets can stay at home in familiar surroundings. That way, pets aren't exposed to sick animals, and they get daily exercise and individual attention. Pet sitters' fees are usually about the same as kennels and boarders. This makes pet sitting a desirable and cost-effective alternative for pet owners.

While pet sitting is an exciting and rewarding career, it is important to remember that it takes time to build a successful business. You might have to work a second job until you build up your client list. Good marketing and customer service skills will help you build a strong business.

Veterinarians

What Veterinarians Do

Veterinarians are doctors who treat sick and injured animals. They also give advice on how to care for and breed healthy animals. Veterinarians treat dogs, cats, and other pets. Some also work with farm and zoo animals such as horses, pigs, sheep, zebras, bears, and chimpanzees.

Veterinarians may be employed by schools and universities, wildlife management groups, zoos, aquarium, ranches, fish

EXPLORING

- Read books and publications about careers in veterinary science. Here are a few suggestions: *ER Vets: Life in an Animal Emergency Room*, by Donna M. Jackson (Houghton Mifflin Books for Children, 2009); *Careers With Animals: Exploring Occupations Involving Dogs, Horses, Cats, Birds, Wildlife, and Exotics*, by Ellen Shenk (Stackpole Books, 2005); and *Exploring Careers: Veterinarian*, by Peggy Parks (KidHaven Press, 2004).

- Visit the American Veterinary Association's Web site (http://www.avma.org) for more information about the field.
- Learn as much as possible about animals.
- You may be able to find volunteer work on farms, in small-animal clinics, pet shops, or animal shelters.
- Extracurricular activities, such as 4-H clubs, offer opportunities to learn about the care of animals.

DID YOU KNOW?

- The first veterinary journal, *De Arte Veterinaria*, was published by Flavius Vegetius Renatus in A.D. 300.
- The first school of veterinary medicine was opened in 1762 in Lyons, France. It was a French immigrant who established the practice of veterinary medicine in the United States almost 100 years later.
- The first agricultural college to establish a veterinary school was Iowa State University in 1879.
- More than 40 percent of horse, or equine, veterinarians are female, according to the American Association of Equine Practitioners.

farms, pet food or pharmaceutical companies, and the government (mainly in the U.S. Departments of Agriculture, Health and Human Services, and Homeland Security). Most, however, work for veterinary clinical practices or hospitals.

Most veterinarians work with small animals that people keep as companions, such as dogs, cats, and birds. They perform surgery, treat minor illnesses, and board both sick and healthy animals that need a temporary place to stay. Sometimes they make emergency house calls, but most veterinarians try to keep normal business hours. Some veterinarians may work as many as 60 hours a week if emergency health problems occur.

Other veterinarians work with larger animals or may even work with both large animals and small house pets. Some of these doctors specialize in the treatment and care of animals such as horses, cattle, and sheep. Others specialize in treating fish or poultry, such as ducks and geese.

In small towns or in the country, veterinarians may travel long distances to treat animals. Some large cattle ranches or horse farms keep veterinarians on their staff. Most zoos also employ a full-time veterinarian to manage the health care, feeding, and treatment of their entire animal population.

A veterinarian at an animal hospital examines the ear of a Brittany spaniel.
(C S. Cannerelli, Syracuse Newspapers/The Image Works)

Many veterinarians work as inspectors in the food industry, such as in meat-packing and chicken-processing companies. They examine the meat for signs of disease.

To be a successful veterinarian, you should be very good at science. You should also have lifelong interest in scientific learning as well as a liking and understanding of animals. Good communication skills will help you interact well with pet owners and coworkers, as well as write reports.

It is important for aspiring veterinarians to realize that pet illnesses and injuries cannot always be healed. In these instances, an animal may have to be euthanized (that is, humanely killed). These situations can be sad and stressful, but vets have to be strong in order to help the pet owner deal with his or her grief and feeling of loss.

Education and Training

To work as a veterinarian, you must have a doctor of veterinary medicine (D.V.M.) degree. You must also pass a state licensing board exam plus one or more national exams. You need at least

Veterinarian Practice Areas, 2008

Practice Area	Percentage of Vets
Companion Animal Exclusive	67.3 percent
Companion Animal Predominant	9.9 percent
Mixed Animal	7.3 percent
Food Animal Predominant	6.7 percent
Horse	6.1 percent
Food Animal Exclusive	1.8 percent
Other	1.0 percent

Source: American Veterinary Medical Association

FOR MORE INFO

For career information, contact
Academy of Rural Veterinarians
90 State Street, Suite 1009
Albany, NY 12207-1710
877-362-1150
arv@caphill.com
http://www.ruralvets.com

For information on veterinarians who treat horses and job shadowing, contact
American Association of Equine Practitioners
4075 Iron Works Parkway
Lexington, KY 40511-8483
859-233-0147
aaepoffice@aaep.org
http://www.aaep.org/index.php

For information on veterinary careers in zoos, contact
American Association of Zoo Veterinarians
581705 White Oak Road
Yulee, FL 32097-2169
904-225-3275
http://www.aazv.org

For more information on careers, schools, and veterinary resources, contact
American Veterinary Medical Association
1931 North Meacham Road,
Suite 100
Schaumburg, IL 60173-4360
847-925-8070
avmainfo@avma.org
http://www.avma.org

For information on educational programs, contact
Association of American Veterinary Medical Colleges
1101 Vermont Avenue, NW, Suite 301
Washington, DC 20005-3539
202-371-9195
http://www.aavmc.org

six years of college after graduation from high school to earn a D.V.M. degree. Most accredited schools of veterinary medicine in the United States offer four-year programs, and most require you to complete at least two years of general college courses before you enter the veterinarian program. Some junior colleges offer preveterinary training.

Many preveterinary students earn a bachelor's degree from a four-year college before they apply for admission to the D.V.M. degree program. It is very hard to get into veterinary school. You typically must have grades of "B" or better, especially in the sciences.

Earnings

Veterinarians who specialized in large animal care earned average starting salaries of $62,424 in 2008, according to the American Veterinary Medical Association. Those who specialized in treating small animals, such as dogs or cats, averaged $64,744. The average starting salary for all veterinarians was $48,328.

Veterinarians earned an average salary of $75,230 in 2007, according to the U.S. Department of Labor. Veterinarians with many years of experience in the field earned $134,920 or more.

Outlook

Job prospects will be very good for veterinarians in coming years. More people have pets these days, and many are willing to pay to make sure that they remain healthy. There will be a shortage of veterinarians who specialize in public health, research, and food supply veterinary medicine. Veterinarians who treat farm animals in rural areas will also be in strong demand. Many people do not want to work in rural areas, so there is a shortage of veterinarians in these positions. Competition will be stronger for veterinarians who treat small animals, such as dogs, birds, and cats.

Veterinary Technicians

What Veterinary Technicians Do

Veterinary technicians help veterinarians care for animals. During routine exams, veterinary technicians restrain animals, clean ears, and clip nails. They take care of equipment and other supplies and make sure they are in stock. Veterinary technicians take and develop X rays, test for parasites, and examine samples taken from the animal's body, such as blood or stool. About 50 percent of a veterinary technician's duties involve laboratory testing. They make careful notes, write reports, and enter information on computers.

In clinics or private practices, veterinary technicians help with surgical procedures. This generally means preparing the

EXPLORING

- Read books about veterinary science.
- Visit the American Veterinary Association's Web site (http://www.avma.org) for more information about the field.
- You may be able to volunteer at kennels, animal shelters, zoos, or

training schools. Volunteer work may not involve direct contact with animals until you are older, but it is a good opportunity to be in an animal-care environment.
- Ask your guidance counselor to arrange an information interview with a veterinary technician.

A veterinary technician steadies a three-day-old giraffe. (Elise Amendola/ AP Images)

DID YOU KNOW?

Where Veterinary Technicians Work

- Veterinary clinics
- Animal hospitals
- Zoos
- Aquariums
- Colleges and universities
- Farms
- Research laboratories
- Military service
- Humane societies
- Veterinary supply sales

animal for surgery by shaving the incision area and applying an antibacterial medicine to the skin. Surgical anesthesia is administered and controlled by veterinary technicians. Throughout the surgery process, technicians keep track of the surgical instruments and watch the animal's vital signs. If an animal is very ill and has no chance for survival, veterinary technicians may have to help euthanize it. Veterinary technicians may also assist the veterinarian in trying to determine the cause of an animal's death.

Veterinary technicians should be able to interact well with a variety of people. In clinical or private practice, it is usually the veterinary technician who explains treatment and subsequent animal care to the animal's owner. Technicians may have to help euthanize an animal that is very sick or severely injured and cannot get well. As a result, they must be emotionally stable and help pet owners deal with their grief and loss. Other important traits for veterinary technicians include punctuality, the ability to follow instructions, and good organizational and time-management skills.

Education and Training

Take courses in science, computers, chemistry, math, and health in high school. Get any experience with animals that you can.

After high school, you must graduate from a two-year program that is accredited by the American Veterinary Medical Association. There are also some four-year programs that lead to a bachelor's degree. These programs include courses in chemistry, mathematics, communications, medical ethics (how to make the right decisions regarding medical care), computers, nutrition, medical terminology, veterinary anatomy, and clinical procedures, such as radiography. You also receive practical training working with live animals.

Earnings

Veterinarian technicians just starting out in the field earn less than $19,000. Those with advanced education and experience can make more than $50,000 a year. Veterinary technicians who work for zoos and research facilities earn higher salaries than those who work for veterinarians in private practice or veterinary clinics. The U.S. Department of Labor reports that veterinary technicians earned the following mean annual salaries by type of employer in 2008: federal government, $44,790; scientific and research organizations, $39,830; colleges and universities, $35,550; and social advocacy organizations, $27,720.

> ## Web Sites for Vet Techs
>
> **GoodNewsforPets**
> http://www.goodnewsforpets.com
>
> **The Pet Center**
> http://www.thepetcenter.com
>
> *Veterinary Technician*
> http://www.vetlearn.com

Outlook

Very strong employment growth is expected for veterinary technicians in the next decade. The veterinary care industry is stable even in weak economic times. Animals will always need care, and pet owners are willing to pay for care even if they are cutting other expenses. Most people consider their pets as a member of the family. There will be a steady demand for qualified technicians as the number of people who own pets continues to grow. Opportunities will also be good for veterinary technicians in research and rural practice areas. Competitions

FOR MORE INFO

For more information on veterinary technician careers, contact the following organizations:

Academy of Veterinary Emergency and Critical Care Technicians
6335 Camp Bullis Road, Suite 12
San Antonio, TX 78257-9721
210-826-1488
http://www.avecct.org

American Association of Equine Veterinary Technicians and Assistants
http://www.aaevt.com

Association of Zoo Veterinary Technicians
c/o Roger Williams Park Zoo
1000 Elmwood Avenue
Providence, RI 02907-3655
http://www.azvt.org

For more information on careers, schools, and veterinary resources, contact
American Veterinary Medical Association
1931 North Meacham Road, Suite 100
Schaumburg, IL 60173-4360
847-925-8070
avmainfo@avma.org
http://www.avma.org

For information on veterinary specialties, visit the association's Web site.
National Association of Veterinary Technicians in America
50 South Pickett Street, Suite 110
Alexandria, VA 22304-7206
703-740-8737
info@navta.net
http://www.navta.net

for jobs in aquariums and zoos will be very strong because many people want to work in these positions. Opportunities will be best for veterinary technicians with advanced education and many years of experience in the field.

Wildlife Photographers

What Wildlife Photographers Do

Wildlife photographers take photographs and make films of animals in their natural environment. The photographs are used in science publications, research reports, textbooks, newspapers, magazines, and many other printed materials. Films are used in research and for professional and public education. Photographs and films are also used on Web sites and in e-books and e-magazines.

Wildlife photographers often find themselves in swamps, deserts, jungles, at the tops of trees, in underground tunnels,

EXPLORING

- Take classes in photography, media arts (film, sound recording), and life sciences.
- Join photography clubs or enter contests that encourage you to use camera equipment.
- Learn how to use different types of film, lenses, and filters.
- Learn how to use a digital camera. See "On the Web" on page 84.

- Practice taking pictures of birds and other animals at parks, nature centers, and zoos.
- Watch nature shows and videos to learn more about both animal behavior and filming animals in the wild.
- Read books and magazines about animals—especially those that feature photographs of animals in their native habitat.

On the Web

Visit the following Web sites to learn how to photograph wildlife and natural areas:

HOW TO PHOTOGRAPH WILDLIFE LIKE A PRO
http://www.travellady.com/Issues/
November08/5359photograph.htm

PHOTOGRAPHY BASICS
http://www.photography-basics.
com/page/4

WILDLIFE RESEARCH PHOTOGRAPHY
http://www.moosepeterson.com/home.
html

swimming in the ocean or hanging from the side of a mountain. They may shoot pictures of the tiniest insects (such as the red headed ash borer) or the largest mammals (such as the blue whale).

Some wildlife photographers focus on one family or species or in one region or area. For example, some wildlife photographers may shoot chimpanzees in their various habitats in Africa—from humid forests to savanna-woodlands. Another photographer might shoot various species of birds that live in the southwestern United States, such as the roadrunner and elf owl.

Like other professional photographers, wildlife photographers must know about light, camera settings, lenses, film, filters, and digital photography. In addition, they must be able to take pictures without disturbing the animals or natural settings that they photograph. To do this, they must learn about the animals and plants they use as subjects before they go into the wild. For example, they must know how close they can get to a buffalo before it might get mad and charge them, and what plants, such as poison ivy, might cause them discomfort if touched.

All photographers should have manual dexterity, good eyesight and color vision, and artistic ability. They should be patient since it may take hours or even days to take just the right photograph. Self-employed (or freelance) photographers need good business skills. They must be able to manage their own studios, including hiring and managing assistants and other employees, keeping records, and maintaining photographic and business files. Marketing and sales skills are also important for successful freelance photographers.

Wildlife photographers do not necessarily need to be zoologists, although a background in biology or zoology is helpful for this career. After many years of experience, wildlife photographers often become experts in the behavior of the animals they photograph. It is also possible for zoologists who use photography in their research to eventually become expert wildlife photographers.

The technological advances in photography and the expertise of wildlife photographers have contributed much to scientific knowledge about animal behavior, new species, evolution, and animals' roles in preserving or changing the environment.

Wildlife photographers are employed by publishing companies, television stations (such as Animal Planet), nonprofit agencies, government agencies (such as the National Park Service and the U.S. Fish & Wildlife Service), and any other organization that requires photographs or videos of wildlife and nature.

Tips for Taking Wildlife Photos

- Study the animals you want to photograph before you go out. Learn about their eating, sleeping, and other behaviors so you will know what to expect.
- Plan ahead and take the right kind and amount of film you need (or extra digital storage if you use a digital camera). Consider the light and weather conditions. Take extra camera batteries.
- Wear dark clothes that blend in with surroundings.
- Don't stand where you will stick out like a sore thumb. Stay in shadows near trees or shrubs.
- Keep your distance.
- Be patient and alert. While you are waiting to take a photo or shoot film of a particular animal, you may see dozens of other opportunities to shoot other birds, insects, and animals around you.

FOR MORE INFO

For information on accredited photography programs, contact

National Association of Schools of Art and Design
11250 Roger Bacon Drive, Suite 21
Reston, VA 20190-5248
703-437-0700
info@arts-accredit.org
http://nasad.arts-accredit.org

For information on nature photography, contact

North American Nature Photography Association
10200 West 44th Avenue, Suite 304
Wheat Ridge, CO 80033-2840
303-422-8527
info@nanpa.org
http://www.nanpa.org

For information on photography careers, contact

Professional Photographers of America
229 Peachtree Street, NE,
Suite 2200
Atlanta, GA 30303-1608
800-786-6277
http://www.ppa.com

For articles about a career in photography, visit the society's Web site.

Student Photographic Society
229 Peachtree Street, NE,
Suite 2200
Atlanta, GA 30303-1608
866-886-5325
info@studentphoto.com
http://www.studentphoto.com

Some wildlife photographers are employed as teachers at colleges and universities, while still operating a freelance business in their spare time.

Education and Training

There are no formal education requirements for becoming a wildlife photographer. It's a good idea, though, to earn at least a high school diploma to prepare for this career. Earning a college degree is even better. A degree will help you learn about both photography and biology. A bachelor of arts in photography or film with additional classes in biology would prepare you well for a career as a wildlife photographer. While in school, you should try to gain practical experience and build a portfolio of your work. A portfolio is a collection of your best work.

Wildlife photographers must not risk the well-being of any animal to take a picture. They must show concern for the environment in their work. They must use common sense and not anger or frighten any animals while trying to take a picture.

Earnings

Full-time wildlife photographers earn salaries that range from about $19,000 to $41,000 a year. Most wildlife photographers work as freelancers. Wildlife photographers who combine scientific training and photographic expertise usually start at higher salaries than other photographers. It can be hard to earn a living as a wildlife photographer. You may have to earn additional money by working in another job or do other kinds of photography until you become known for your work as a wildlife photographer.

Outlook

Employment of photographers in all fields is expected to be steady. The demand for new photographs and videos of animals in their natural habitats should remain strong. Researchers, book and magazine editors, and television stations all need photographs and videos of wildlife. It is important to remember that only a small number of people work as full-time wildlife photographers. People who know a lot about nature and digital photography will have the best job prospects.

Zoo and Aquarium Curators and Directors

What Zoo and Aquarium Curators and Directors Do

Curators and directors work as managers in zoos and aquariums. They supervise employees, animals, and business operations.

Curators are experts in the daily care, medical plans, diet, social habits, and habitats (areas where animals normally live) of the animals in their care. They work closely with zookeepers, veterinarians, exhibit designers, and teachers. They develop exhibits, educational programs, and visitor services. They manage the daily activities of assistant curators, zookeepers, administrative staff, researchers, students, and volunteers. They oversee important research that shows whether the animals' activities, habitats, and diets are the best they can be. Zoo and aquarium curators also keep inventories of animals, attend scientific and research conferences, prepare budgets, and write reports.

Curators work with other institutions, too. For example, they might share research information or arrange to loan an animal to another zoo for breeding. (Breeding is the sexual pairing of two members of the same species for the purpose of producing offspring.) Curators oversee purchases from animal dealers, and arrange for collection of nonendangered species from the wild.

Large zoos and aquariums often have a general curator to oversee the entire collection of animals, plus a curator for each division. For instance, a large zoo might have a general curator, a bird curator, a reptile curator, and a mammal curator. General curators work closely with the zoo or aquarium director and other members of the staff to make long-term plans and develop policies that will keep the facility running smoothly.

Zoo and aquarium directors' jobs are like those of company presidents or school principals. They are responsible mainly for the important business affairs of their institutions. Directors are in charge of all the institution's operations. They develop long-range plans, start new programs, and oversee the animal collection and facilities. Directors of public zoos and aquariums usually report to a governing board, a group of people who set policies and make rules for the institution, such as how money is spent. Directors make sure those policies and rules are followed.

EXPLORING

- Read books and journals on animals and nature.
- Visit the following Web sites to learn more about animals: Animal Diversity Web (http://animaldiversity.ummz.umich.edu), Animal Fact Guide (http://www.animalfactguide.com), and Seaworld: Animals (http://www.seaworld.org).
- Volunteer at animal shelters, zoos, kennels, pet stores, stables, veterinary facilities, or anywhere you can get experience working directly with animals.
- Visit your local zoos and aquariums often. Attend events and educational programs they offer.
- Join clubs, such as 4-H or National FFA Organization, to help you learn about animals.
- Ask a teacher or school counselor to arrange an information interview with a curator or director.

DID YOU KNOW?

How Zoos Get Their Animals

Zoos buy most of their animals from regular dealers who collect them from all over the world. Sometimes a zoo will send out its own collecting expedition. Animals are also obtained by trading with other zoos. Animals that are hard to collect and transport, or that are difficult to breed in captivity, are the most expensive. Lions are relatively inexpensive animals because they are easy to breed and raise in zoos. White rhinoceroses are among the most expensive.

Directors plan budgets based on fund-raising programs, government grants, and private donations. Directors of larger zoos and aquariums may give speeches, appear at fund-raising events, and represent their organizations on television or radio. A major part of the director's job is seeing that the zoo or aquarium has enough money. Directors also spend a great deal of time working with architects, engineers, contractors, and artists on renovation and construction of facilities, exhibits, and other projects.

Directors inform the public about what is going on at the zoo or aquarium. They talk to reporters, write annual reports, and write articles for newsletters, newspapers, and magazines. Directors also may work on committees for conservation organizations or with universities and scientists to support conservation research.

Education and Training

If you are interested in becoming a curator, you should take high school courses in the sciences (biology, zoology, etc.), mathematics, computer sciences, language, and speech.

After high school, you need to earn at least a bachelor's degree in one of the biological sciences, such as zoology, ecology, biology, mammalogy, or ornithology. A master's or doctoral degree is often required to work in large zoos or aquariums.

In addition to advanced education, it takes years of on-the-job experience to learn about animal husbandry (the care and breeding of animals). Many curators start out by volunteering as zookeepers and work their way up over the years, getting experience at the same time as earning their degrees.

To become a zoo or aquarium director, you need a well-rounded education. In high school, you should take classes in zoology, biology, accounting, economics, and general business. Courses in sociology, speech, and debate will improve your ability to speak to the public and to reporters, as well as talk with governing boards and staff members. You will also need to earn at least a bachelor's degree in business management or administration. Most directors have master's degrees. Many directors in larger institutions have doctoral degrees. A background in both science and business will make you a desirable candidate for employment.

Earnings

Salaries for zoo and aquarium curators and directors depend on the size and location of the facility, whether it is privately or publicly owned, the size of its budget, and the worker's responsibilities, educational background, and experience.

Yearly salaries for curators can range from a low of $20,000 to more than $80,000. General curators in large cities earn average salaries of around $55,000.

Zoo and aquarium directors earn anywhere from $30,000 to $100,000 or more a year. A few directors in large metropolitan areas earn $150,000 or more.

Outlook

There will be few openings for zoo and aquarium curators and directors in the next

Tips for Success

To be a successful zoo and aquarium curator or director, you should

- love animals and care about their welfare
- be able to get along well with people
- have strong management skills
- have leadership abilities
- have good oral and written communication skills
- be organized

FOR MORE INFO

Visit the association's Web site to read about careers in the field.

Association of Zoos and Aquariums
8403 Colesville Road, Suite 710
Silver Spring, MD 20910-3314
301-562-0777
http://www.aza.org

For general information on careers and marine mammals, contact

Alliance of Marine Mammal Parks and Aquariums
ammpa@aol.com
http://www.ammpa.org

decade. There are only about 215 professionally operated zoos, aquariums, wildlife parks, and oceanariums in North America. Each employs only one director and three to five curators. Competition for these jobs will be extremely strong. Workers with advanced education and experience in zoos or aquariums will have the best job prospects. There are also opportunities in foreign countries, including those, such as the United Kingdom, New Zealand, and Australia, where English is spoken.

Zookeepers

What Zookeepers Do

Zookeepers are the daily caretakers of zoo animals. They prepare the animals' diets, clean and maintain cages, and watch animals' behavior. They give vitamins or medications to the animals. They

EXPLORING

- Most zoos and aquariums have Web sites that offer information about their programs and career opportunities. Visit http://www.aza.org/FindZooAquarium for links to zoos and aquariums. Another site to visit for career information is the Saint Louis Zoo's So You Want to be a Zookeeper? (http://www.stlzoo.org/animals/soyouwanttobea-zookeeper).
- Many zoos and aquariums offer classes about animals and conservation. They also offer volunteer opportunities, such as Explorers or Junior Zookeeper programs.

- Volunteer duties may include cleaning enclosures, preparing food, or handling domesticated animals (an animal that has been kept and raised by humans). Contact a zoo near you to learn what programs are offered.
- Watch nature shows on television.
- Watch wildlife in parks and in other natural settings. Keep a journal that details what you see.
- You may also find volunteer opportunities at animal shelters, boarding kennels, wildlife rehabilitation centers, stables, or animal hospitals.

Tips for Success

To be a successful zookeeper, you should

- have a strong love of animals
- not mind getting dirty while doing your job
- be able to follow instructions
- be very observant in order to tell when animals are sick or angry
- have good communication skills
- be detail oriented
- be able to work both independently and as part of a team
- have good judgment
- be able to react well under pressure

fill water containers in their cages and safely move animals from one location to another. Zookeepers provide enrichment devices for the animals. These might include ropes for monkeys to swing on, scratching areas for big cats, blocks of ice that contains frozen fish for polar bears, or new branches or bridges for chimpanzees and other animals to climb and cross. Zookeepers also might add simulated prey items to exhibits to encourage animals to engage in natural stalk-and-chase behaviors. They regulate environmental factors, such as temperature and humidity, and wash and groom animals.

Zookeepers work closely with other zoo staff on research, conservation (the practice of preserving natural resources, including animals), and animal reproduction (the sexual pairing of two members of the same species for the purpose of producing offspring). They also talk to zoo visitors. They give them information and answer questions about the animals they care for. Sometimes zookeepers have to keep visitors from teasing or feeding the animals.

Zookeepers have many custodial and maintenance tasks. These can be physically demanding and dirty. They must deal with live food items and body wastes. They must work both indoors and outdoors, in all kinds of weather. Zookeepers sometimes face the risk of injury and disease.

Keepers often work with one particular group of animals such as primates or birds, but in some zoos (usually smaller ones) keepers may care for a wide range of species (a group of related organisms that are capable of breeding). Zookeepers become experts on the species and the individual animals in their care. They observe and understand eating, sleeping, mating, and social habits. They notice even small changes in animals' appearance and behavior so that any illness or injury can be taken care of right away.

Education and Training

Take math and science (biology, ecology, chemistry, and botany) classes in high school. For entry-level zookeeping positions you need a college degree. Degrees in animal science, zoology,

A zookeeper writes a report detailing the care of two giant tortoises. (Barry Batchelor/Press Association Wire/AP Images)

Zoos in History

People have put wild animals on display since ancient times. About 1500 B.C., Queen Hatshepsut of Egypt established the earliest known zoo. The Chinese emperor, Wen Wang, founded a zoo that covered about 1,500 acres around 1000 B.C. The ancient Greeks established public zoos, while the Romans had many private zoos.

During the Middle Ages, zoos became rare in Europe. But by the end of the 1400s, European explorers returned from the New World with strange animals, and people once again became interested in zoos. A fantastic zoo, with 300 keepers taking care of birds, mammals, and reptiles, was created in Mexico in the early 16th century by Hernando Cortes, the Spanish conqueror. During the next 250 years, a number of zoos were established. Some were small collections of bears or tigers kept in cramped cages or pits. They were gradually replaced by larger collections of animals that received better care.

Today, most zoos are cageless and try to create homes for the animals that look and feel like their natural habitats.

marine biology, conservation biology, wildlife management, or animal behavior are the best choices. A few colleges and junior colleges offer a specialized curriculum for zookeepers. Animal care experience, such as zoo volunteer work or veterinary hospital work, is important.

Some major zoos offer formal zookeeper training courses, as well as on-the-job training programs. These programs are available to students who are studying fields related to animal science and care. Participation in these programs can lead to full-time positions as zookeepers.

Earnings

Most people who choose a career as a zookeeper do not do so for the money, but because they feel compassion for and enjoy being around animals.

Salaries vary widely among zoological parks and depend on the size and location of the institution, whether it is publicly or privately owned, the size of its endowments and budget, and whether the zookeepers belong to a union (union workers usually earn higher salaries than those who are not members of a union). Salaries also vary by zookeepers' education and experience level. Zookeepers earn salaries that range from just above minimum wage ($7.25 an hour) to more than $40,000 a year. Zookeepers who work at zoos in large cities usually earn the highest salaries.

Outlook

There are only about 215 professionally operated zoos, aquariums, and wildlife parks in North America. Only a small number of jobs become available each year. This will make it hard to start a career in the field. Zoos are becoming more involved in animal preservation. There will be a growing need

FOR MORE INFO

For general information on careers and marine mammals, contact
Alliance of Marine Mammal Parks and Aquariums
ammpa@aol.com
http://www.ammpa.org

Visit the association's Web site to read the online pamphlet, Zoo Keeping as a Career.
American Association of Zoo Keepers
3601 29th Street, SW, Suite 133

Topeka, KS 66614-2054
785-273-9149
http://www.aazk.org

For information about careers, contact
Association of Zoos and Aquariums
8403 Colesville Road, Suite 710
Silver Spring, MD 20910-3314
301-562-0777
http://www.aza.org

for zookeepers to work in preservation of endangered species (a species that has so few individual survivors that it may die off). They will also be needed to educate the public about conservation.

Zoologists

What Zoologists Do

Zoologists are biologists who study animals. They usually specialize in one animal group. *Entomologists* are experts on insects. *Ornithologists* study birds. *Mammalogists* focus on mammals. *Herpetologists* specialize in reptiles. *Ichthyologists* study fish.

EXPLORING

- Learn as much as you can about animals on the Internet. Here are a few suggestions: Animal Corner (http://www.animal-corner.co.uk), Oakland Zoo: Animals (http://www.oakland-zoo.org/animals), and Yahoo!: Kids: Animals (http://kids.yahoo.com/animals).
- Read books and other publications about animals. Here are a few suggestions: *Endangered Animals*, by Rhonda Lucas Donald (Children's Press, 2002); *National Geographic Encyclopedia of Animals*, by Karen McGhee and George McKay (National Geographic Children's Books, 2006); and *Wild Science: Amazing Encounters Between Animals and the People Who Study Them*, by Victoria Miles, Martin Kratt, and Chris Kratt (Raincoast Books, 2004).
- Explore hobbies such as bird-watching, insect collecting, or raising hamsters, rabbits, and other pets.
- Offer to pet sit for your neighbors. This will give you a chance to observe and care for animals.

Tips for Success

To be a successful zoologist, you should

- be fascinated by animals
- be curious
- enjoy working outdoors in all types of weather
- be willing to work long hours
- have the ability to do more than one task at a time
- be willing to continue to learn throughout your career
- enjoy reading and writing
- be able to work well with others

Some zoologists specialize even more. They focus on a specific part or aspect of an animal. For example, a zoologist might study single-celled organisms, a particular variety of fish (such as the Green Back Cutthroat trout), or the behavior of one group of animals, such as elephants, owls, or orangutans.

Some zoologists are primarily teachers. Others spend most of their time doing research. Nearly all zoologists spend a major portion of their time at the computer. Most zoologists spend very little time outdoors (an average of two to eight weeks per year). In fact, junior scientists often spend more time in the field than senior scientists do. Senior scientists coordinate research, supervise other workers, and try to find funding. Raising money is an extremely important activity for zoologists who work for government agencies or universities. They need the money to pay for research and fieldwork.

Basic research zoologists conduct experiments on live or dead animals, in a laboratory or in natural surroundings. They make discoveries that might help humans. Such research in the past has led to discoveries about nutrition, aging, food production, and pest control. Some research zoologists work in the field with wild animals, such as whales or wolves. They trace their movements with radio transmitters and observe their eating habits, mating patterns, and other behavior. Researchers use all kinds of laboratory chemicals and equipment such as dissecting tools, microscopes, slides, electron microscopes, and other complicated machinery.

Zoologists in applied research use basic research to solve problems in medicine, conservation, and aquarium and zoo work. For example, applied researchers may develop a new drug for people or animals. Others may invent a new pesticide or a new type of pet food. (A pesticide is a substance, often made from chemicals, that is used to stop a pest—an animal, insect, or other organism—from hurting plants or animals.)

Many zoologists teach in colleges and universities while they do their own research. Some zoologists manage zoos and aquariums. Still others work for government agencies, private businesses, and research organizations.

Education and Training

Science classes, especially in biology, are important if you want to become a zoologist. You should also study English, communications, and computer science.

DID YOU KNOW?

- The world's largest dog on record was an Old English mastiff, named Zorba. He weighed 343 pounds and was 8 feet 3 inches long from nose to tail.
- The smallest dog on record was a Yorkie from Blackburn, England, who was 2.5 inches tall and 3.75 inches long. He weighed only 4 ounces.
- The world's smallest cat on record was a male Blue Point Himalayan-Persian named Tinker Toy. He was 2.75 inches tall and 7.5 inches long.

- The cheetah is the fastest land animal. It is the only cat that cannot retract its claws.
- The world's largest bird is the male African ostrich. They have been recorded to measure 9 feet tall and weigh 345 pounds.
- The world's smallest bird is the adult male bee hummingbird of Cuba. It is 2.24 inches long and weighs 0.056 ounces.

Source: Amazing Animal Facts

FOR MORE INFO

For information about a career as a zoologist, contact

American Institute of Biological Sciences
1444 I Street, NW, Suite 200
Washington, DC 20005-6535
202-628-1500
http://www.aibs.org

For information about all areas of zoology, contact

Society for Integrative and Comparative Biology
1313 Dolley Madison Boulevard, Suite 402
McLean, VA 22101-3926
800-955-1236
http://www.sicb.org

After high school, you must go to college to earn a bachelor's degree. A master's or doctoral degree is usually also required. You do not need to specialize until you enter a master's degree program.

Earnings

Zoologists earned average salaries of about $55,000 a year in 2007, according to the U.S. Department of Labor. Beginning salaries for those with a bachelor's degree in biological and life sciences were $34,953, according to the National Association of Colleges and Employers. Zoologists who worked for the federal government earned average salaries of about $69,630.

Outlook

Employment for zoologists is expected to be good in coming years. This is because there is more interest in protecting and studying animals. But since this field is small, there will be a lot of competition for research jobs.

Glossary

accredited approved as meeting established standards for providing good training and education; this approval is usually given by an independent organization of professionals

annual salary the money an individual earns for an entire year of work

apprentice a person who is learning a trade by working under the supervision of a skilled worker; apprentices often receive classroom instruction in addition to their supervised practical experience

associate's degree an academic rank or title granted by a community or junior college or similar institution to graduates of a two-year program of education beyond high school

bachelor's degree an academic rank or title given to a person who has completed a four-year program of study at a college or university; also called an *undergraduate degree* or *baccalaureate*

career an occupation for which a worker receives training and has an opportunity for advancement

certified approved as meeting established requirements for skill, knowledge, and experience in a particular field; people are certified by the organization of professionals in their field

college a higher education institution that is above the high school level

community college a public or private two-year college attended by students who do not usually live at the college; graduates of a community college receive an associate's degree and may transfer to a four-year college or university to complete a bachelor's degree

diploma a certificate or document given by a school to show that a person has completed a course or has graduated from the school

distance education a type of educational program that allows students to take classes and complete their education by mail or the Internet

doctorate   the highest academic rank or title granted by a graduate school to a person who has completed a two- to three-year program after having received a master's degree

freelancer   a worker who is not a regular employee of a company; they work for themselves and do not receive a regular paycheck

fringe benefit   a payment or benefit to an employee in addition to regular wages or salary; examples of fringe benefits include a pension, a paid vacation, and health or life insurance

graduate school   a school that people may attend after they have received their bachelor's degree; people who complete an educational program at a graduate school earn a master's degree or a doctorate

intern   an advanced student (usually one with at least some college training) in a professional field who is employed in a job that is intended to provide supervised practical experience for the student

internship   1. the position or job of an intern; 2. the period of time when a person is an intern

junior college   a two-year college that offers courses like those in the first half of a four-year college program; graduates of a junior college usually receive an associate's degree and may transfer to a four-year college or university to complete a bachelor's degree

liberal arts   the subjects covered by college courses that develop broad general knowledge rather than specific occupational skills; the liberal arts are often considered to include philosophy, literature and the arts, history, language, and some courses in the social sciences and natural sciences

major   the academic field in which a college student specializes and receives a degree

master's degree   an academic rank or title granted by a graduate school to a person who has completed a one- or two-year program after having received a bachelor's degree

pension   an amount of money paid regularly by an employer to a former employee after he or she retires from working

scholarship   a gift of money to a student to help the student pay for further education

social studies   courses of study (such as civics, geography, and history) that deal with how human societies work

starting salary   salary paid to a newly hired employee; the starting salary is usually a smaller amount than is paid to a more experienced worker

technical college   a private or public college offering two- or four-year programs in technical subjects; technical colleges offer courses in both general and technical subjects and award associate's degrees and bachelor's degrees

undergraduate   a student at a college or university who has not yet received a degree

undergraduate degree   see **bachelor's degree**

union   an organization whose members are workers in a particular industry or company; the union works to gain better wages, benefits, and working conditions for its members; also called a *labor union* or *trade union*

vocational school   a public or private school that offers training in one or more skills or trades

wage   money that is paid in return for work done, especially money paid on the basis of the number of hours or days worked

Browse and Learn More

Books

Donald, Rhonda Lucas. *Endangered Animals.* New York: Children's Press, 2002.

Heitzmann, William Ray. *Opportunities in Marine Science and Maritime Careers.* New York: McGraw-Hill, 2006.

Hollow, Michele C., and William P. Rives. *The Everything Guide to Working with Animals: From Dog Groomer to Wildlife Rescuer- Tons of Great Jobs For Animal Lovers.* Cincinnati, Ohio: Adams Media Corporation, 2009.

Jackson, Donna M. *ER Vets: Life in an Animal Emergency Room.* Boston: Houghton Mifflin Books for Children, 2005.

Libal, Joyce. *Rural Teens and Animal Raising: Large and Small Pets.* Broomall, Pa.: Mason Crest Publishers, 2007.

McAlary, Florence, and Judith Love Cohen. *You Can Be a Woman Marine Biologist.* Rev. ed. Marina del Rey, Calif.: Cascade Pass Inc., 2001.

McGavin, George C. *Endangered: Wildlife on the Brink of Extinction.* Richmond Hill, Ont.: Firefly Books, 2006.

McGhee, Karen, and George McKay. *National Geographic Encyclopedia of Animals.* Washington, D.C.: National Geographic Children's Books, 2006.

McKay, George. (ed.) *The Encyclopedia of Animals: A Complete Visual Guide.* Berkeley, Calif.: University of California Press, 2004.

McMillan, Beverly, and John A. Musick. *Oceans.* New York: Simon & Schuster Children's Publishing, 2007.

Miles, Victoria, Martin Kratt, and Chris Kratt. *Wild Science: Amazing Encounters Between Animals and the People Who Study Them.* Vancouver, B.C., Canada: Raincoast Books, 2004.

Miller, Adam. Body Doubles: *Cloning Plants and Animals.* 2nd ed. Chicago: Heinemann-Raintree Library, 2009.

Needham, Bobbe. *Ecology Crafts For Kids: 50 Great Ways To Make Friends With Planet Earth.* New York: Sterling Publishing, 1998.

Newkirk, Ingrid. *50 Awesome Ways Kids Can Help Animals: Fun and Easy Ways to Be a Kind Kid.* Rev. ed. Boston: Grand Central Publishing, 2006.

Parks, Peggy. *Exploring Careers: Veterinarian.* Farmington Hills, Mich.: KidHaven Press, 2004.

Pasternak, Ceel, and Linda Thornburg. *Cool Careers for Girls with Animals.* New York: Scholastic, 2000.

Peterson's. *Peterson's Summer Opportunities for Kids & Teenagers.* 26th ed. Lawrenceville, N.J.: Peterson's, 2008.

Ritter, Christie. *Animal Rights.* Edina, Minn.: Abdo Publishing Company, 2008.

Shenk, Ellen. *Careers With Animals: Exploring Occupations Involving Dogs, Horses, Cats, Birds, Wildlife, and Exotics.* Mechanicsburg, Pa.: Stackpole Books, 2005.

University of California Press. *The Atlas of Endangered Species.* Berkeley, Calif.: University of California Press, 2008.

Van Tuyl, Christine. *Zoos and Animal Welfare.* Farmington Hills, Mich.: Greenhaven Press, 2007.

Weil, Zoe. *So, You Love Animals: An Action-Packed, Fun-Filled Book to Help Kids Help Animals.* Gabriola Island, B.C., Canada: New Society Publishers, 2004.

Periodicals

Friends of the Earth Newsmagazine
http://www.foe.org

Kids' Corner
http://www.akc.org/public_education/kids_corner/kidscorner.cfm

National Geographic Adventure
http://www.nationalgeographic.com/adventure

National Geographic Explorer
http://magma.nationalgeographic.com/ngexplorer

National Geographic Kids
http://kids.nationalgeographic.com

National Parks
http://www.npca.org

Nature Conservancy
http://www.nature.org/magazine

Ranger Rick
http://www.nwf.org

Sierra
http://www.sierraclub.org/sierra

Zoobooks
http://www.zoobooks.com

Web Sites

About.com: Environmental Issues
http://environment.about.com/mbody.htm

American Camping Association: Find a Camp
http://find.acacamps.org/finding_a_camp.php

American Kennel Club: Kids/Juniors
http://www.akc.org/kids_juniors/index.cfm?nav_area=
kids_juniors

American Library Association: Great Web Sites for Kids
http://www.ala.org/greatsites

American Veterinary Association: Care for Animals
http://www.avma.org/careforanimals

Animal Corner
http://www.animalcorner.co.uk

Animal Diversity Web
http://animaldiversity.ummz.umich.edu

Animal Fact Guide
http://www.animalfactguide.com

Animaland
http://www2.aspca.org/site/PageServer?pagename=kids_home

Association of Zoos and Aquariums
http://www.aza.org/ForEveryone/CareersKids

Backyard Nature
http://www.backyardnature.net

BBC Science & Nature
http://www.bbc.co.uk/nature

Canon Envirothon
http://www.envirothon.org

CanopyMeg.com
http://www.canopymeg.com

Careers in Aquatic and Marine Science
http://www.aqua.org/downloads/pdf/Marine_Science_Careers.pdf

Careers in Forestry & Natural Resources
http://www.forestrycareers.org

Careers in Oceanography, Marine Science, and Marine Biology
http://ocean.peterbrueggeman.com/career.html

EcoKids
http://www.ecokids.ca

Environmental Education for Kids!
http://www.dnr.state.wi.us/eek

Exploratorium
http://www.exploratorium.edu

Exploring Nature Educational Resource
http://www.exploringnature.org

The Green Squad
http://www.nrdc.org/greensquad

Insectclopedia
http://www.insectclopedia.com

The Jane Goodall Institute
http://www.janegoodall.org

kids4research
http://www.kids4research.org

KidsCamps.com
http://www.kidscamps.com

Kids Go Wild
http://www.kidsgowild.com

Kids: Pet Care
http://www.spca.bc.ca/kids/animalcare

Kids' Planet
http://www.kidsplanet.org

Magic Porthole
http://www.magicporthole.org

MarineBio
http://www.marinebio.com

National Audubon Society
http://www.audubon.org/educate/kids

National Park Service: Interpretation and Education
http://www.nps.gov/learn

National Park Service: Nature and Science
http://www.nature.nps.gov

National Wildlife Federation
http://www.nwf.org/kids

Oakland Zoo: Animals
http://www.oaklandzoo.org/animals

The Pet Center
http://www.thepetcenter.com

Petpourri

http://www.avma.org/careforanimals/kidscorner/default.asp

Preparing for a Wildlife Career

http://nationalzoo.si.edu/Education/WildlifeCareers

PBS: American Field Guide

http://www.pbs.org/americanfieldguide

Sea Grant Marine Careers

http://www.marinecareers.net

Seaworld: Animals

http://www.seaworld.org

Sierra Club

http://www.sierraclub.org

Underground Adventure

http://www.fieldmuseum.org/undergroundadventure

U.S. Fish & Wildlife Service

http://www.fws.gov

World Wildlife Fund

http://www.worldwildlife.org

Yahoo!: Kids: Animals

http://kids.yahoo.com/animals

zootoo

http://www.zootoo.com

Index